Jamie Edwards

D1078129

ISBN 978-09-55159-31-2

Published by:
Trained Brain Media, Clifton House, Range Lane, Denshaw,
Saddleworth, OL3 5SA

Mental Ketchup: The Source of Peak Performance

Jamie Edwards

trainedbrain.
M E D I A
www.trained-brain.com

What they say about Jamie Edwards

"I have always been a sceptic! The thought of needing anyone else to help me sort out my own issues would in my mind make me weak. Jamie changed my perception. He helped me understand me better and he gave me the techniques which have helped improve my mental state before and during games. Ultimately he has made me a better player."
Lewis Moody MBE, Leicester Tigers & England

"With over 12 years' experience in the personal development field I have had the privilege to work with and attend some of the world's most powerful and communicative speakers, and in my opinion Jamie is one of the most outstanding speakers I have heard."
Elliott Wald, Published Author, Personal Development Coach & Speaker

"What Jamie Edwards delivers best is clarity. His training and insight provide elite athletes, managers, leaders and decision-makers with a mental tool-box that unlocks the door to clear-thinking, confidence and self-belief. I've been lucky enough to observe him working in close-quarters with all of the above and his methods are especially applicable and successful in high-pressure environments when another axis-shifting moment is only a second away."
Ben Wyatt
Director, Communications, Europe
SONY ERICSSON WTA TOUR

"Full of fantastic methods to keep any serious player on the right track before, during and after their matches."
Dan Bloxham, Head Coach All England Tennis Club

Dedicated to Nicola, Kobe and Marnie and all those who helped train my brain.

Acknowledgements

They say there is no 'I' in team and the same is true in both sports and in life. We play the game of life on different teams and in somewhat different leagues throughout our time here. My parents played a huge supporting role in the development of my trained brain. Mike, my uncle was instrumental in stretching me, challenging my thinking early on, when it really mattered. The coaches I played for over the years have shared valuable lessons both on and off the courts where I plied my trade along with my associates and friends, all of whom have had a hand in my development in some way. The individuals I am indebted to are far too many to mention by name but I have been influenced by many who were not professional coaches but had, nevertheless, many great lessons to teach.

Having played competitive basketball two mentors passed on their wisdom to me from the age of 14 onwards. Cleave Lewis was one of the most unassuming players in the UK. At 6'6" he didn't go unnoticed on the basketball court physically but he had this way of surprising the opposition with his under-the-radar abilities, his way of looking at the game and what went on on the court provided me with many insights. My other sporting mentor was Alton Byrd and was not so much under the radar as squarely on the radar screen. In fact the paradox of Cleave Alton Byrd, a British basketball legend remains to this day. He was only 5'9" tall and you would think he'd be unseen, lost in a game which is designed to favour giants. But playing a game for giants Alton stood out physically in a way that was extremely hard to ignore. Both he and Lewis however had a common thread. They stood out mentally. In a game where apparently, height, reach and endurance, not to mention speed and agility, count, they played above the odds and outperformed the opposition because they used what few others did: their brain.

The ability of the mental, invisible and unseen aspect of the 'game', and I am using the term here figuratively to include every aspect of human activity from sports performance to business deals, to influence the visible, tangible aspects is exactly what this book is about.

We use ketchup to spice things up. To release rather than hide flavours in our food and to create tastes which are more than just the sum of their parts.

Mental ketchup is no different. When all other things are equal what you learn to apply here will help you stand out from the crowd and achieve more than even you thought was possible.

In addition to dipping in and out of this book you will find that there is a page at the end of each chapter for you to scribble your own thoughts and ideas that may have been triggered by a relevant point. There are two questions I always get a client to ask: How does this apply to me? How do I take action? When you ask these two questions at the end of the chapter you will find where you can start adding your own mental ketchup.

Asking good questions leads to good answers. Many times you have tried something in the past so the real question should be at the end of the chapter "Did I learn something new or was I reminded of something I have forgotten?" In either case jot it down in the space provided.

If you are really ready to spice up your game, in whatever walk of life this might be, dip in here, apply mental ketchup and get ready to enjoy the experience.

Table of Contents

What's your sauce?

I was asked not so long ago what I put on my meals when I was younger. The topic of conversation was sauces or condiments. Mustards, ketchup, brown sauce, mint sauce all came to mind. The rich array of flavours that are added to our favourite meals around the world are all different. The commonality is that sauces are there to add something to what you already have, to spice it up, to change it in small but important ways and to create a taste experience which makes the ordinary extraordinary. A sauce is not always added. Sometimes you choose to use it and at other times you think you decide you can do with out it.

One of my earliest memories of my favourite sauce goes back to my Nana's signature meal: Chicken and Rice. I remember seeing an uncle put a drop of ketchup on the side. "That's different," I thought.

Performance in life is no different. If your sauce was a mental skill where would you add it? My mentors early in my sports career always emphasized their counsel could be applied to many areas of life not just the sporting arena. In fact they all emphasized that the applications of these skills were better served away from sports which were, many times, by definition carried out in a limiting, narrowly focused environment.

Do you know where you could add mental skills to your performances in sports, business and life? Sometimes it's obvious where and why you need to add something to what you are doing. Many times it's not. But over the years I have had the privilege to work with some elite and aspiring athletes as well as some very switched on business executives and entrepreneurs who in their own way discovered what their source of peak performance is, their 'sauce' in effect. Most of the time the reaction was: "It's so obvious. Common sense really." But it's obvious only with the power of hindsight. As Moshe Feldenkrais referred to it's what we call the 'elusive obvious' and it usually eludes us which is why a detached, professional view can help us so much in finding what we need.

My goal with this book is to share with you some of the tools and ideas that I have used and tested in the unforgiving world of sports. The fact that most people only look at how they think when something is going wrong is a challenge in itself to any coach.

Used to seeing people who come to me only as a result of their reacting to the environment or situation which is no longer going their way it is music to my ears when someone comes to me and says "Nothing wrong with me. I want to develop these tools. I want to have them in place, just in case."

It's rare because our culture often tells us that there must be something wrong with us if we ask someone about the state of mind we find ourselves in. There have been many clients who, after it was suggested that they look at the mental aspect of their game, I know said to their agents, coaches, managers or even parents. "There's nothing wrong with me. I'm not mad!" There is a lot of truth in that statement. We are not mad. The challenge is that there is usually something missing from the performances we are putting in week in week out. The raw ingredients are all there but when it comes to putting it all together there is something missing from the final result. It is ok, but it is less than the sum of its parts would have it be. It needs some spicing up. It needs a sauce.

What is in the sauce? *Your* sauce?

Your sauce may not be 'ketchup' but you have definitely tasted something different in those days when everything was so effortless and your performance was not just flawless but bordered on the sublime. It's like adding a sauce to a meal. Sometimes it goes unnoticed. Even if the performances are at another level. You may be curious to find out what were the exact ingredients to that success and try to replicate them.

Martin Seligman, the renowned psychologist who wrote the book *Authentic Happiness* was asked what was wrong with psychology. The state of psychology he said was: A. It was good. B. It was not good. or C. It was not good enough.

For many years the science of the mind especially in the context of sports and business was content with looking for "What is wrong?" For every study on happiness there were several more on depression. If you look for what is wrong in life or in a situation you often find something wrong with it, the inevitable rule of finding fault does not fail to apply, especially here, in this context. Fifty years ago the development of neuro sciences led to the miserable being made to feel less miserable. But while this helped those who were at a stage where help is exactly what they needed, there were no skills or tools to help us develop and build on strengths as well as weakness. There was no easy way to prepare for further development.

Today in every arena of life you will find that it is

next to impossible to go to another level, compete at a higher plane or be even more successful in what you do than you are now, you will need to critically examine the way you think.

In this book you will find my passion for the mental game and my desire to make the advice which will help you usable, practical and applicable to your own personal life or game.

We are not reinventing the wheel here. There are a lot of clues which have been left behind by those that went before us. There are many clues we can use to help us achieve real results and many of these clues point to the fact that the answers we seek are usually within. They are never too far away. Just like that favourite sauce that you had on the table or in the cupboard, they are always within reach, we just need to recognise them.

At this point I need to stress that there is a subtle difference between eating and tasting. Most people actually wolf their food down and hardly taste it. Their mind is elsewhere missing the actual joy of the process. Similarly, 'tasting' the sauce of peak performance is difficult if you have infused it with combinations which create inner conflict and contradictions which prevent you from getting where you want to be.

Awareness requires different skills in order to achieve a different attitude. This is not change. By being able to look at things differently you see things you could not see before. Awareness is a key mental skill. Can you distinguish the difference between the mindset you are in and the mindset you need? Do you understand your own mind? Just like being aware of what you are eating allows you to enjoy the different flavours which make the experience a pleasure, your mental taste buds will be sharper when you slow down and take notice of how you think. *Mental Ketchup* is designed to help you get more flavour out of life. It has been written in a way which will allow you to internalise what you learn and apply it to your activities.

Enjoy dipping in and out of the many pages that follow and get ready to take your performance to brand new levels.

Jamie Edwards, Manchester, 2009.

Chapter One

Potential

> *"The control center of your life is your attitude."*
> *-Norman Cousins*

If I hear the word 'potential' once in the business of performance coaching I hear it a million times. I often ask at seminars "who has had that word attached to them?" Many have at some point in their life because we all have potential. The question is *do we all use it*? And again most of my listeners agree that potential is something that is often underused. We have glimpses of it in brief flashes. The potential ebbs and flows like the tide and it brings us great delight in what we believe is possible and how the future can be so different and then the waves of talent ebb as the tide goes out in the distance and we are often found seeking, floundering in our attempt to recapture the experience, again.

It is this seeking that causes the illusion that there is something to find. That there is something hidden from you or us which needs to be 'discovered' and its discovery will provide the answers we need. The truth is that really nothing is hidden and if we look closely at what, where and why, we are usually sitting on top of the very aspects we are looking for. This means that in order to perform better the first step is to stop seeking and first start undoing.

Update or be Obsolete

Imagine if you were to run your business, go about keeping in touch with friends and colleagues by email or wanted to look at the latest blog or needed to research a topic of interest but it was on a computer that was running Windows '98. Do you remember Windows '98? I do. I thought it was everything. I was amazed at what it could do. Yet if you were still using that software to run your PC today you would experience a lot of anger and frustration. It would make life difficult, you wouldn't be able to perform at the level you wanted to and imagine what the communication would be like at the other end. Your friends, family and business associates wouldn't be able to get through to you.

You would, in short, be blocked, conflicted and frustrated with your inability to perform at the level you want no matter how hard you try.

Today there are many who have not updated their software and are living and playing the game of life with the mental equivalent of Windows '98. So it's time to update that software. How many times does your current laptop or desktop ask and suggest there is an update available? Wouldn't it be great if your mind had the ability to do this also?

We know so much about IT today. It has advanced

tremendously over the past 5, 10, 15 and even 20 years at a pace which is truly breathtaking. What we can do today is out of this world, literally, and that is where it is taking us. The development of information technology is occurring at such a speed that there is always the risk that if we but blink we will be out of date, our knowledge and skills made obsolete.

How much has you HT or Human Technology advanced in the same period of time? Have you developed your HT at the same rate? If not will you let both the HT and IT move on at the same speeds?

If you are 30 years old you have on this earth approximately 262,080 hours. If you are 40 years old you have been here on this earth 349,440 hours.

See the chart below:

AGE	20	30	40	50
Hours	174,720	262,080	349,440	436,800

That is a lot of hours and it is a lot of hours of either good or poor conditioning. We have been conditioned by our environment, by family, by the establishment and by those who have influenced us and by those we have chosen to hang out with in the past or keep company with today. We are bound to be influenced by future acquaintances we have not even met yet. We are who we hang out with or said differently we will be become who we consistently hang out with.

Many of our skills, beliefs, ideas, rituals, thought processes and identities have either knowingly or unknowingly become part of us through a process of moulding through our interaction with others. They have been trained like an athlete is trained or a specific sporting skill is conditioned with constant repetition.

Who taught you?

I want you, at this point, to consider who trained you. Who and where did you have your early influences? The good, the bad and the ugly ones. Whose software did you download as a young man or woman looking to make strides in the world?

A friend of mine once called this 'Grandad Training' because if it came from your dad there is a chance that your granddad pasted it onto him. Not always, but he certainly found that his training came from there. Now depending on who your parents are or your grandparents will determine what type of training you received as a child. The children of Donald Trump will have had access to a certain type of training in life. His experience in building companies, brands, negotiating, dealing with adversity have all been part of his life and style and it will have rubbed-off on his family because, inevitably, we tend to take our 'style' with us into our family and personal life.

So Donald Trump's children will have received a different type of training than the daughter of a politician would have or the children of the local estate agent and likewise the children of Michael Jordan will have had access to a certain type of training in their life which would have been unique to their environment because of their father. They will have the benefit of his many years of experience of competing in the world of professional sports, dealing with the lifestyle his fame brought as one of the legends of modern sport and learning to cope with the complexities and challenges this produces.

There is no right or wrong in this process. Depending on the experiences of our parents, grandparents or even the community we were raised in our upbringing will have had an impact on our mental game. The question is to really identify, here, who trained you. What did you learn, how did you learn it and more importantly how have you applied that training in your life so far?

The question we are trying to establish is if you need to update, which will then lead us naturally to: Who from and from where? There is no standing still with this because your own software at some point in your life will be reminding you...."Updates available" If you haven't had that reminder (or at least a sense that you need to do something in order to raise your game a notch or two) then maybe you should start to ask that question at the start of this paragraph.

Personal Growth

The one obstacle in the game of life is playing the 'Blame Game'. A game that has impacted all of us and can limit our progress in so many areas of life. The blame game is nothing but excuses.

Excuses are nothing but well planned lies which halt progress because they create a false sense that somehow you are not responsible for your own 'upgrade'. This is not true. The truth, as the saying goes, will set you free. Honesty about where you find yourself is the initial step required in training your own brain. It is very easy to blame events in your life for getting you where you are now. The fact is however that there is an event in everyone's life.

As you probably guessed in my professional life I get to come across more than my fair share of excuses and, as a result, I become inured to them.

It will help you understand just how easy it is for us to use excuses when you read some of the following that get bandied around:

"If I didn't have a spouse or family stopping me.."
"If I had enough 'pull'…"
"If I had money…"
"If I had a better education…"
"If I had good health…"
"If my partner hadn't left me…"
"If other people understood me…"
"If conditions around me were different…"
"iIf I could live my life over again…"
"If I didn't fear what they would say…"
"If I had only been given a chance…."
"If I now had the chance…"
"If I could only do what I want…"
"If I was younger…"
"If others didn't have it in for me…"
"If I had been born rich…"
"I never seem to meet the right people…."
"If I had the same equipment …"
"If I had the talent that some people have…"
"If I took hold of that opportunity…"
"If I didn't have to look after the children…"
"If I could save some money.."
"If my boss appreciated me…"
"If I lived in a big city…"
"If I weren't so fat…"

"If I could just get a break.."
"If I hadn't failed.."
"If luck was not against me.."
"If only I had my own business…"
"If my family understood me.."
"If I could just get started…"
"If my talent was known"
"If I didn't have a past…"
"If other people would listen to me…"
"If I'd have only performed in the audition…"
"It was because of the coach that I didn't have the chance to play."
" My boss didn't like me."

A partner leaves a relationship, there is a divorce in the family, a loved one passes away. The company you work for has to lay you off. There are events in our lives upon which we can blame any amount of failure. Everyone has them. They are commonplace (even though at a personal level, when they happen they are still traumatic). These are also the excuses which allow you displace blame from yourself to other elements. Blame is also thrown at people in your life. Blame is a crutch which stops you from standing on your own two feet. Blame is an excuse.

What I will say now may sound harsh but you are not reading this book in order to be told lies which will make you feel good. You know that the time has come to take charge of your life. You are, right now, thinking honestly about yourself and your situation. So let's face it: "Excuses are the crutches of the untalented".

The types of excuses we have just read about are fatal to your progress because they keep you playing the blame game which keeps you locked up in the past. Blaming people, the events that inevitably happen or even beating up on yourself keeps you stuck in a rut.

When you are in a situation which is not quite going your way you always have two options. The first is to play the blame game (that's the easy one).

The second option is for you to change any situation or condition that you find yourself in. This takes courage, it takes faith and it takes inner strength because as human beings we are not comfortable with change. Change is and always will be scary. It isn't the change itself we are afraid of however, it is the uncertainty and the unknown. But if you don't know what lies ahead, logic dictates that you should just go ahead and make the change, right?

No, that doesn't usually happen. So this step involves changing your current circumstances. It was Einstein who said "the definition of insanity is doing the same thing over and over again and expecting different results."

Taking Einstein's definition I know we all suddenly know a lot of insane people. The power to change is always inside us. The ability to change is what becomes the leader within us.

Next step if you cannot change the circumstances, is to change your beliefs. Change your current view point or beliefs about what has happened in your life and what is happening in your life, sports, business. Whatever it is. If you are going to access more of that potential then focussing on better questions will help you define what all of this means to you.

What is interesting to me is the way people make

their decisions. Not so much why they make some decisions but how they make them. I am always intensely interested in what is most important to them at a certain moment in time and how does that change from a minute to an hour, a few days, a few weeks or even a few months.

What we think and believe in can change and it can change based on the following factors:

Factors which affect your thinking:
1. events
2. people
3. places
4. time

It will help you in your own self-analysis if we look at each of these in turn.

EVENTS: The events in our lives can have a huge impact on our thinking. Going over the past can help because it allows us to examine the events which have shaped us, not just negatively but also positively. This is why you must be prepared when you mentally go over the past not to lay blame but think of some of the events in your life which have shaped you, your environment and what you believe in.

PEOPLE: We have all met someone who has helped us with a career, a dilemna, someone who has turned our world upside down, swept us off our feet or given us the nugget of information we needed at just the right time.

There is an old oriental saying which states that "When the student is ready the teacher will appear."

People shape our lives and in turn those people can positively or negatively influence the way we think.

Focus on the people who have shaped your life. Analyse exactly what it was they did or said. How this impacted upon you and what you believe the effect is now.

TIME: To a greater or lesser extent we are all products of our times. The times we live in are a huge impact on the mindset and the development of trained brains.

Depending on when your parents were born would have had an influence on their own personal philosophy. In the USA during these times of economic uncertainty the historians are recalling the times of the Great Depression. Those times shaped a generation. If you lived in those times as a young person you wanted to help the nation get back to its feet and a collective mindset was created about rebuilding.

Then came World War II. Consider just how that era shaped the thinking of many countries and left an indelible mark on the psyche of this country? Or you might have been a product of the 'Swinging 60s' and you were brought up with this sense of freedom and a spirit that was about experimentation and social revolution.

The point is that we do not live in a vacuum. The world we live in shapes us in more ways than we care to think and what we really should be thinking or doing for that matter is developing our thinking to precede the conditions of our life. To precede the times, the places, the people so we have some tools to manage what is happening.

In the unforgiving world of sports many of the situations that leave us emotionally drained do so because of the interaction with our favourite sports stars. This despite the fact that the event we experience is indirect and takes place in the (admittedly emotionally charged) atmosphere of a sporting event or the even more removed (but still emotionally charged) comfort of our living room.

Sports conditions: The time of the game, the opponents or people involved including teammates, coaches, fans, agents, all these are elements which can each (or all) have an impact on the way we think and feel.

General events we experience or even a specific event can influence an athlete's thinking. Performing at events such as the Olympics, or in the Ryder Cup, the Ashes or even the Rugby World Cup can change the routines and rituals you have developed as part of your performance due to the different nature, or magnitude, of the event itself and this can have an impact on an athlete's performance.

To illustrate the huge degree of impact the time factor can play think that the sporting times you live and work in can be an influencing factor. Without the advent of global media Jack Nichlaus and Arnold Palmer became golf superstars under the guidance of legendary sports agent Mark McCormick. Yet today, the sporting phenomenon, Tiger Woods has plied his trade and given all mere mortals something to aspire to when on the golf course in a way that neither Nichlaus nor Palmer ever achieved. The impact of Tiger's arrival on the PGA Tour has benefited from the cultural times we live in. The use of media has made him into one of the most marketable commodities in world sport. Yet had he arrived in the 1970's his impact on the game would not be as dramatic and it is even possible his own performance would not be what it is today.

Imagine if you were Barack Obama and you ran for the Presidency 10 years ago. Would he have had the impact he has had now? I don't think so. He has benefited from the times we live in. The American people are ready for change and the power of social networking has had a significant impact on the way they run Presidential election campaigns today.

If you played in the old first division of the English football league and were a superstar back in the day compared to the Premiership stars who grace the nation's TV screens your career would have had a profound change as a result of the times and the sport.

So as you contemplate where you are now think about what is going on in your life right now that is impacting upon your thinking.

It always helps to quantify this so write down a couple of conditions and how they are impacting upon you.

CONDITIONS   THINKING

Times _____   _____

Events_____   _____

People_____   _____

Places_____   _____

Road Blocks

When the thinking precedes the conditions you are starting to give yourself the best chance of fulfilling the potential that has been linked to you. When you look at the conditions of your life and take a different look at them through a different set of eyes as opposed to the same view that you have been looking at all this time you will begin to see what you are really capable of. It is only then that you begin to understand exactly what you would need to do in order to take your performance to the next level.

Let's see some of the practical steps you need to take in order to get your thinking out of the rut.

1. Stop Blaming: It is way too easy to cast blame and it excuses us from what matters most which is moving forward. We blame people, events, and most of all we blame ourselves. This only keeps us engulfed in the past which has created the conditions. In all walks of life the courage comes from acceptance of that situation and then being courageous enough to let go of it.

The good thing about the past is that it is the past and it only keeps dominating your thoughts because of conditioning. You need to realise that it is time for it to stop. Today, is it possible to let go of the past conditions that have affected you. By evaluating them and understanding them you can then, discard them. In that moment when you ultimately decide to let go of the thought that fuels the emotions which influence your thinking and take on a new energy that is required for change you are beginning to make a fundamental change in your own inner psychology.

I am often fond (and for a good reason) of saying: "There is no strength in blame". Blaming others gives us a type of release from the situation because we then feel that our inability to deal with it is justified. The fact is that it is only a temporary release. Blaming events chains you, engulfs the mind in the "if this wouldn't have happened the way it did....things would have been different" kind of mentality and emasculates your ability to affect positive, life-changing, personal, faith-affirming, energising action.

Blame, once we start apportioning it, rarely stops outside ourselves. The real energy drainer is the type of blame where you point the finger of blame right back at yourself. In fact pointing one finger out sends three fingers back. Yet the sooner we are taught, coached or guided to let go of the past the sooner we feel liberated and ready to race off.

You cannot drive a car with the handbrake on. Releasing the brake in your life starts with stopping that process of beating yourself up over a situation you may not have been able to control, or a person's actions which are outside your ability to shape.

2. Change the Conditions: This is the challenge. Change is and it can be scary because as humans we love the familiar, it comforts us and it gives us a false sense of safety. This is something we shall see in the next chapter. Yet at some level we know that life, sports, relationships, career, whatever you want can be improved. You have wanted to change, you want to change, this is the reason you are reading this right now. If your conditions are not as you would like them in the present you do have an option of changing what has been happening.

I know this is a bold statement, one of those which we can easily think that they are easy to say but hard to do. Yet as you examine what you have written when you were detailing the conditions which affect your thinking you will be able to look at the list critically and start to think "What could I change here that would increase the quality of my conditions?"

The moment you decide to change a condition you have impacted upon the present moment and moved yourself on mentally from the past which held you bound. But because the human mind loves repeating patterns it will be afraid of doing anything different.

The unknown, the uncertainty drives us into numerous states of being. The unknown is the unknown and if you haven't done it before then you should in theory get on with it.

Living the NOW

What most people are afraid of is changing their current situation. It isn't going to the unknown it's changing the known that causes fear and uncertainty. And yet the more you can deal with change, the more successful you will be.

Take Tiger Woods for instance; why is he so successful? Because he has the ability to deal with the unknown better than any golfer on the planet. He cannot control a golf ball. That's a myth. He is the best in the world at influencing a golf ball which means that on any given day his ball will decide to make him look ordinary. It happens on rare occasions. One of which was at the 2008 US Open at Torrey Pines. Tiger was incredibly 5 over par for the 1st hole alone in a week where he clearly was struggling with what looked like the type of injury that would have kept most players on the other side of the ropes. He hit it all over the place yet even with the uncertainty of not knowing where the ball was going to end up he found certainty somewhere else: *Inside himself.*

In business you read every day about those iconic figures who have shaped our world by not knowing what it was like on the other side but being courageous enough to change the now, live the now. The inventions from yesteryear can and do represent someone saying: "We need to do something different. We can create a better product," and then going ahead and doing it.

Bill Gates wanted to have a PC in everyone's home. Steve Jobs, the founder of Apple still to this day questions the current safe side of design by bringing innovative new products to the world, changing and challenging current conditions and challenging traditional thinking (and design) in the process. Richard Branson has done the same thing numerous times and continues to do it and even in your own sports, business or life you can take that step towards the unknown and embrace it.

Start by asking "What do I have to lose?" or "What do I have to gain?" These are the two statements that will help you to find the motivation you need to start.

Your Notes:

Chapter Two

Rituals

"Bad habits are like a comfortable bed, easy to get into, but hard to get out of."

-Anonymous

Are we creatures of habit? Whenever I ask that question at my seminars the answer is unequivocally YES! Whether it is business or sports we have this idea that habit dictates our success and our failures in all areas of life. Yet if we are creatures of habit how can we benefit from our habits and develop them so that they no longer hold us back?

Firstly, we have to become aware of what is and just as importantly what isn't working for us. Our automatic pilot seems to run away with itself 'without knowing'. Much of what we do day to day happens without thinking, we are unconscious to our own states of minds, we run our lives trying to do as little analytical thinking as possible.

Just the simple act of brushing your teeth is an example of how much we don't know we do something. This morning you didn't pick the brush up whilst looking in the mirror; (if you are like me I have the cold water tap running at the same time) and say

"Right, to the back, up and down now to the side." Most of us unless we are using a new technique or have a new brush which is really different to any brush we have had before have moved past that conscious thought stage. It is now an automatic process that you don't think about but one which, most importantly, works. The toothbrush incident is but an example. There are many rituals which we carry on with in our life without thinking and which provide specific results.

The same rituals that an athlete has in his pre-game preparation, for example, can be related to you. What are your rituals? Imagine you are making your way to your car to go to an appointment. You search deep in your pockets for the keys, you zap the door lock, pull the door and climb in with a style and panache that is unique to you. It is usually at this point that the automatic pilot takes over. You check you are comfortable, put the key in, check your mirror, find neutral with a little shake of the gear stick, check the handbrake is on by touching it or even pulling it up even more, knowing that it is at maximum, but you do it anyway. The final checks are lightning in speed and involve the turn of the key, clutch, first gear and with unquestioned co-ordination you step on the gas, release the brake and ease off the clutch.

That is a lot of information to take in consciously. Do you remember the first time you started driving? How you had to focus on all of the many checks much like a pilot in a cockpit? It was overwhelming. Now of course you do it automatically but what has remained from those days of confusion is a ritual that you "do without thinking". It is in these rituals that we find the ingredients of success or failure.

Because we do them "without thinking" it becomes evident that if we can establish rituals which will lead to success we will have a better chance at succeeding. This is where we must then ask ourselves the question: "Do my current rituals work? Are they leading me to where I want to be?"

If they are and you are experiencing success in any area of your life, business or sport then the rituals and the patterns must be very good indeed and you should stick to them. If you are not experiencing life as you know it could be, that quiet voice in your head keeps hinting that there is more for you out there then you have to look at changing your rituals in order to get to a new desired result.

Most of us can do something for a few days. You can give up a vice, chocolate in my case for a few days, go to the gym for a few days or weeks, and you can make the change (there is that word again) you need.

Change is logical it is always the result of the need to achieve something. Einstein's dictum cannot apply enough here: "The definition of insanity is doing the same things and expecting different results."

Inside your head, at all times, there is a quiet voice. That quiet voice is the conscious mind. It is very useful at times, like when reading this book but often the conscious mind and the unconscious or subconscious mind get caught up in confusion and work at odds with each other. This leads into internal conflict and inaction as you are not sure which one to listen to.

You have one voice in your head saying "Don't do it, don't do it. You know you will regret it later!" and you have the other voice in your head saying gleefully

"Go on! Just this time!" Which one do you think usually wins? Usually it is this second voice. Why? Because the second voice is the unconscious mind.

Bring to mind something that you have tried and failed to give up in the past. This may have been training at the gym, smoking or a diet. It also works the other way too.

We can all do something for a few days. The question is whether you can keep on doing it so that it becomes a new habit you can benefit from.

Your Notes:

Jamie Edwards

Chapter Three

Hitting the Bullseye

"If you think you can do a thing or think you can't do a thing, you're right."
-Henry Ford

Every person that you come into contact with has (fortunately or unfortunately) an *unconscious mind* as well as the obvious conscious mind. Hitting the bullseye is the ultimate in any type of target practice. The same can be said of communication between the two minds.

This is more than a metaphor. It works well in terms of visualising your mental set up. Imagine that the bullseye represents the unconscious mind and the outer edge of the target circle represents the conscious mind. All the behaviours and habits you develop are stored right at the bullseye of the target. If you want to be even more successful it requires developing the skill to aim at the middle.

Front Desk

Have you ever been to a retail store and wanted to return some goods purchased for which you have a receipt? That is a fairly common and universal experience. Now the young person at the front desk has decided it is your turn to be on the receiving end of their lack of service quality and usually this results in what was meant to be a routine exchange of goods turning out to be a lengthy and often frustrating debate about your rights as a consumer.

You manage to keep your emotions in check and start to think that "maybe I am talking to the wrong person." Not only do you think that but immediately after the words follow: "Can I speak to someone who can make a decision?". The only person in the building that can make a decision is the Manager. The Manager is the decision maker. They can resolve this problem in an instant.

Similarly in our heads, the unconscious mind is the manager. It is the ultimate decision maker. It makes decisions long before the conscious mind tries to justify the decision which has been made.

It is important, at this stage, to understand that the two primary functions of the unconscious mind are to *protect* and *maintain*.

In a nutshell it is hard-wired into us from the days when we roamed around in caves when every time we ventured out into the world it was a question of survival, that when we do something if it proves to be safe and does not literally threaten our lives we should *keep on doing it*!

It protects us from perceived or imagined danger. Think about this: If a fly is coming towards your eye you blink, we react to loud noises outside by flinching (or if we have experienced life in a war zone, by ducking). All these are done instinctively, without thinking and they are protective mechanisms. The same mind is designed to keep us the same as we mentioned earlier. We repeat the same patterns of behaviour. The mind is a pattern recognition masterpiece or PRM. It loves seeking the pattern, it is great at understanding the familiarity present in a specific context. Your temperature is maintained without thinking, you heal from injury and disease without thinking and so this amazing software is always protecting and maintaining you.

Yet it over-protects and it over-maintains where we are and what we are and that is, as we shall see, the problem. Identifying 'the problem' is also good because it means that it also allows us to find an acceptable solution. But first let's go and see why the problem occurs.

Doing its job

The mind's ability to work in this way has often stopped people going for that promotion that they always wanted. Here is an example: A job was made available and involved some public speaking. Unfortunately public speaking belongs in the "couldn't think of anything worse" category as having to stand in front of a group of colleagues or strangers and talk is most people's idea of a nightmare. You find some reasons for not going for it and then justify it later with some sort of logic. Do you know of someone who has ever done that? The working here is the same when the mind stops some men approaching an attractive woman and vice versa. That this occurs we all know so we really need to ask why? The mind, here, is protecting us from something. It is usually, failure or rejection. Maybe a memory from the past. The point is that it is saying don't put me in that situation again. While it is preventing us from 'going for it' it is actually doing its job in protecting the fragility of our ego and general tendency to get hurt by rejection and failure.

And whilst the protection is working its magic it also keeps us stuck where we are at the same time. The end result is that you don't take the job. Yes you have lost out on your chance for a higher wage increase but you tell yourself that it would have meant longer hours and more time away. The focus here is on the negative. Trying to protect us the mind is actually focussing on all the things we do not want to happen rather than the ones we want to happen. I have seen this with a Sales team that I worked with. One of the staff had not broken the £50k per month mark and he was wondering why he was unable to go to the next level no matter how hard he tried. I mentioned the concept of protect and maintain and said that these unseen forces are working whether you like it or not. They conspire to hold you back and they succeed unless you are able to analyse them and take conscious action to counteract them.

Who is cutting you down

In Australia there is a phenomenon known as the Tall Poppy Syndrome. Many Australians are known to have left the country because of it. The tallest poppy always gets cut down first. Said differently, you want to progress your career. You know that you are going to have to do some things to keep on improving that are not going to fit in with the group you are currently hanging out with. This can be your friends, your colleagues or your family or community. In some contexts it can also be a cultural group. These groups can hold you back through a mechanism which factors in rejection from them as an important aspect which you want to avoid. You want to play at another level but cannot seem to let go mentally, something is restricting you. Or even someone doesn't want you to leave. The questions which arise at this level are mostly negative. Let's go and examine but a few:

Why do you want to go to school in that city?
What is wrong with your home town?
You'll never make it there.
C'mon let's go out. Don't practice tonight.
No one from this town ever made it at that college.
Who do you think you are?
You can't do that.

There are many more statements that you would recognise as mental handcuffs. People put these handcuffs on you because they don't want you to leave them and it is usually because they love you too. It is worth bearing in mind that those who try to stop you usually do so with the best intentions in mind. No one, usually, actively wants to cause you harm, yet it all adds up to the 'negative' noise we often get to hear in our head.

A legend

Around 2003, I had the very good fortune of working with snooker legend, Jimmy White, affectionately known as the 'Whirlwind' or by his other nickname which was the "People's Champion". Jimmy had a career that had many ups and downs and was associated with more than a few vices such as betting and drinking he had also provided a lot of entertainment for a generation of fans.

The term 'legend' is overused today but he is truly a legend of his sport. When I met him he was still looking to recreate some of the wizardry around the table that made thousands of people follow his instinctive style of play where he literally sped from shot to shot.

During our very first session in a Manchester hotel I was curious to know why one of the most naturally gifted players of his generation had competed in no less than six World Championship Finals and lost all of them. Jimmy had made the personally aware statement that he had been beaten in two of them and lost four of them.

As we discussed those well documented defeats to Stephen Hendry I asked him "What are the consequences of winning the world championship?" He looked up and replied: "Everything doubles! More money, more gambling." As he started talking of everything in his life doubling he was realising what was happening.

Choking in sports is a protective mechanism. Jimmy's unconscious mind was doing its job. It was protecting him from doubling the many circumstances that made his career colourful. It was maintaining him by keeping him the same for his many fans. If the People's Champion had won the World Championship he would have become the World Champion, not their champion and this means he would not have felt as connected to his fans as he was without winning such an international title.

This happens in many other sports. Golfer Greg Norman had thrown away a commanding final day lead in the 1996 Masters at Augusta, succumbing to pressure. Ultimately losing like this is about being comfortable. Comfortable can also be winning if you allow yourself to create the right reasons for it. Many practitioners of sports performance often refer to moments of peak performance as 'being in the zone'. This is a crucial concept so we will look at this next.

Which Zone Are you in?

The comfort zone isn't about comfort. The truth is that we are not designed for success. This is something that many years ago I coached about. The reality is that we have opportunities to be successful but we are not designed for it. We are designed for comfort. Yes, our mind loves comfort. Do you think that record breaking Olympian's Michael Phelps' success is comfortable? Think of the gruelling physical training required and the mental strength needed to repeat what he accomplished. That isn't comfort. The rise to success of Formula 1 star Lewis Hamilton didn't happen by chance nor the many years of success Roger Federer has enjoyed at the top. The business successes that you read about every year about people who have shaped the communities we live in are on the same par. Do you think they are about being comfortable? Overcoming wanting to stop requires strong motivation. Being afraid of failure, being afraid of rejection, not wanting to be poor, these are all motivations any of which (or even a combination of some) could be driving those successes. These motivations (and the rationalisation which occurs once they are accepted) are the *manager* that is being communicated to.

Think about the success of the worker who wants to retrain and develop another career or increase his employment opportunities and studies extra hours on returning home from his 9 to 5 job and has to go to night school or further education. That isn't comfort.

We are designed for comfort and must overcome the urges of the mind to fall back into old patterns in order to experience success.

Beware which zone you are in. Later we will explore *the* zone that you often hear about but for now we shall look at how progress to the next level is made.

Find a new team to play on

Progress comes from stretching yourself beyond what you ever thought was possible. If you are going to find the next level start looking for teammates who are playing the type of game you want to play and who are playing at a higher standard than you are currently playing at. If you play with players of the same standard you will ultimately get only as good as they are.

I refer to it as a game because life is a game. To be enjoyed, it has to be competitive at times and you have several teams and coaches that you come across in your time here that will help you to play the game in a certain way. There are also leagues in life and business just like in the sporting world. These leagues you play in are dependent not just on your ability but the level at which you feel comfortable playing at.

Your Notes:

Jamie Edwards

Chapter Four

Influence

*"Setting an example is not the main means of influencing
another, it is the only means."*
-Albert Einstein

The No 1 skill in life is that of influence. The ability to influence ourself first and foremost. Getting yourself to do something is influence and motivation and resisting something is also influence. What has always interested me in the area of human potential is what are the decisions that someone makes at a certain time and why they make those decisions.

My own son Kobe is like many three and half year olds suddenly acting to become the head of the household and in many cases succeeding I might add. How the times have changed in parenting. My generation and certainly anyone who is over the age of 40 wouldn't have dared to negotiate with their parents about what they were wearing or what time they could go to bed or what colour Nike trainers they were having next. My son is a great example of influence and negotiation.

When he chooses not to participate in an activity like 'tidy-up time' finishing his meal or going to bed he makes it clear and begins a bargaining process. The quality of any communication will depend on how successful we are.

Do we use the 'Carrot' or the 'Stick' methods. Influence is a matter of the right tool in the right moment and what works in one context may not work in another. That goes for yourself not just others.

Let's say you are struggling with getting to the gym or finishing a project. I offer you £5,000. Depending on the size of your bank account you will find a way to get the job done and complete the task. I point a gun to your head and threaten to pull the trigger, I think you will find a way to get the job done no matter what. So the tools of influence should be many. If you only have a hammer to do the job, then you will treat everyone as a nail. As parents to a toddler today we need a toolkit which comprises of carrots and sticks and a few sweets and cakes in between.

Your Notes:

Chapter Five

What business are you in?

"No one can make you feel inferior, without your own consent."
-Eleanor Roosevelt

The competitive world today demands difference, uniqueness and especially in a world that is overly the same, the ability to stand out from the crowd. From brands competing for the attention of a consumer group or a sports team competing for the hard earned entertainment budget of a family to the individual or leader in a coaching role. Everyone is vying for someone's attention even if it's only for a split second.

The process of training the brain starts with what I would term "the ME". Before any coaching process I have to look at what is it that I bring to the relationship. This simple process of ME starts with a question. A question that only the leader can answer.

March of 2007 I was asked to speak at the annual conference for the Professional Golf Association of Sweden. This was a unique trip at the time because no one in the history of the association, which is regarded as one of the best in the world at developing golf coaches and elite players, had before delivered a session like the one I had that day. This is an association whose work is especially notable since the country's population is relatively small and it is dark and covered with snow for a good portion of the year! They do a good job at producing elite performers such as former world number one, Annika Sorenstam.

As I considered what my theme for the conference was going to be the and what message I wanted the coaches to go away and why this question popped into my head... "What business are you in?"

I asked it to myself. I asked it again and again and again. "Coaching, Performance, results, making money, education, entertainment, sports, the list went on and on. Then it occurred to me: "CHANGE!" That's it! *Change*. So I thought what would a coach or a leader say? Yes, they would give the same stock answers that I gave. The logical ones rather than the essence of what had just occurred to me.

The Business of Change

Whatever profession you may be in, whatever your walk of life you are, really, in the business of change. Let us examine what this entails:

BELIEFS: The business of changing your own and those of others.

PERCEPTIONS: Your work requires you to change your perceptions and regardless of your position in life or business there are perceptions that have to be changed against your business or ideas.

ATTITUDES: If you are involved with people then attitude or mindset will affect their performance. With good attitude you tend to get good results. With poor attitude you are setting yourself up for poor results.

STATES: Most importantly to change states or literally how you and others feel. Everything we do we do to change how we feel. That is the result we are all after.

The *ME* approach suggests that it starts with "ME". You look at your own beliefs, your own perceptions, your attitude towards the person in front and monitor your own state of mind.

Consider how all this applies to you and consider, are you in the business of changing beliefs?

Communicating to the unconscious mind is a skill. One that is either learned from experience, trial and error or one that is trained through a number of disciplines in the world of neurosciences that are available today.

Change and influence take part at the deeper level of the mind. The part that I refer to as the bullseye. When coaching an athlete, my own work is defined by this metaphor. One that captures the imagination and more importantly the heart and emotion of someone who competes for a living.

What type of pen are you?

Let's take a Parker pen as an example which will illustrate what I mean. So let us choose a Parker pen at a value that would start from £7 onwards and let's also take a very popular, more common, pen as a comparison metric. Imagine now you have a BIC pen with a value of approximately 20p. Finishing off the list you will have the complimentary free hotel pen too. Now can you imagine that I use these to draw a black line on a flipchart with each of the pens. Then imagine that I pull out of my pocket my Mont Blanc. Value approximately: £150. Then I throw the following question out to the audience: Can you tell the difference between the quality of the lines?

Given just the drawn lines to go with, certainly not, despite there being a difference of £149.80p between the Mont Blac and the BIC pen. You cannot tell the difference between the Parker and the really cheap pen in terms of quality just by the line I drew on the flipchart either.

The example is transferable. Let us make you a pen in your world. You write lines, make your mark in the business and social world. You also tell the story of your life. You are a pen. The difference between the pens, though they all do the same job is that the Mont Blanc stands out from the crowd. It has a different casing, its owner will pay that bit more and the reason why is because of *perceived value*.

The Mont Blanc has a perceived value that the others don't. What is your perceived value in your company, with your team and even in your family. How do you stand out in the 'sea of sameness'? These are the questions you need to ask yourself (and answer honestly) in order to arrive at a clearer picture of who you are.

Your Notes:

Jamie Edwards

Chapter Six

The Two Big Lies

> *"If nothing in your life is going right, turn left."*
> *-Anonymous*

> *"The only difference between a rut and a grave is their dimensions."*
> *-Ellen Glasgow*

Positive thinking is a lie. I am going to repeat this just in case you missed it (and because emphasis, right now is important). Positive thinking is a lie. My own experiences coaching mental skills to performance and celebrity sports stars are not based around positive thinking. By its very nature positive thinking is misleading. As the leader in your own life one of the most important and bravest decisions you could make is to stay open to the *possible*. Let me explain this by using a sporting example.

Imagine a golfer who has a 6ft putt. He approaches the putt with a very positive state of mind. He says to himself "I'm going to make this!" with conviction. He has picked the intended line the ball is going to roll on. His technique is effective due to hours of repetition and the cushion of certainty that hours and hours of practice give to any performer. He's about as positive as it is humanly possible to be. The question asked at this stage is, "Will the golf ball definitely go in the hole?" and the answer is that no, it will not definitely go in the hole.

This is exactly why positive thinking is a lie. By being positive and not getting the outcome you want it can often lead to the exact opposite effect in your mind which is being negative, which on the flip side of the coin our golfer definitely does not want to be.

By feeling negative he hasn't practiced all week and he has been down on himself regarding his golf progress and lack of good putting opportunities. Most people when they have tried to be very positive in their thinking and outlook often find that they oscillate between being happy and being sad.

Now let's reverse the situation a little. Let us imagine our golfer being a little less than diligent. He may have been too busy partying, for example, to prepare all week. His technique is not where he wants it to be and he has the thought chains of "I'm going to miss. I missed the last two putts," going through his mind. He knows that in terms of preparation he does not deserve to win. He has no idea of where to start the ball rolling and doesn't feel confident about his game, yet he does not stop being a golfer. The question here again is… "Will he definitely miss?"

You are correct in identifying that here, again, there is no cast-iron guarantee you can give me that the golfer will definitely miss (unless he decides to throw the game that is) so now we get into the interesting situation of seeing how the mind is being lied to. One instant you say it's going in and the next you say it is going to miss and neither carries any more element of truth in it than the other. The truth, instead, is found within one of the most important words in the English language: Possible.

Now if we are to approach the exact same situation, facing the same challenge in each case and pose the question with the mindset of what is possible we would actually come a lot closer to the truth of what may or may not happen.

"Is it possible that I could hole the next putt? Yes. Do I definitely hole it?…No. Do I definitely miss? Not at all. Yet is it possible I could make this putt? Yes, and that is the truth.

Possible isn't about positive or negative thinking, it is something which I call neutral thinking.

Some leaders in sports and business will have a natural way of creating a neutral mindset. Yet coaching 'Neutral Thinking' to your team mates or sending out the message is all that is needed to give your clients a valuable mindset for moving from the present (where they are right now) into the future (where they want to be). As you can imagine there is a formula that could very well help you in sports, business and life. As someone who is curious you are primarily involved in the process of *change*, this means that a technique, an attitude or a routine can be responsible for an instant change in fortunes.

POSSIBLE: In his book *Extraordinary Golf: The Art of the Possible*, Fred Shoemaker said the bravest thing a player can do is stay open to the possible. This is the difference between positive thinking and negative thinking. If you can deal with the consequences then having positivity is a contributor to success in life and being a leader. I believe leaders have neutrality about their thinking skills. They have the ability to deal with what happens in sports, business and life. This comes about because they have a clear way of looking at things. What I would call clarity of vision (clarity for short) and which we will look at next.

CLARITY: The intention answers the questions. Why and what is the outcome you are after? Most have developed the habit of asking for what they don't want. That would be like walking around the supermarket with a shopping list of everything you didn't want. Your behaviour would be quite erratic as you would have to spend time zeroing in on products you did not want to buy in order to avoid them before you could even get to the ones you are actually looking for. Clarity of vision is vital to acting with purpose.

ACTION: once you have achieved the clarity of vision required and have a perfect picture in your head you have to take action. Thinking isn't enough. After you have stated your intention the next step is that you have to then take the action necessary to make it happen. Thinking isn't enough.

RESULT: Every action that you take is going to produce a result. It is here that you must be aware of what I call the "crazy 8 or the loop of insanity."

When someone is stuck in a mindset of negative emotions or a feeling of helplessness it tends to show at this point. The result isn't quite what you wanted, a missed putt, the deal didn't quite work out the way you hoped, the meeting was a disaster. Whatever the situation where a result didn't work out you will find yourself looping back to the step above.

This is usually preceded with a global question of "What did I do wrong?" The question immediately has the mind search for what didn't work. The old adage that if you look for what is wrong you will find it is definitely applicable here.

When the golfer or sportsman (or businessman for that matter) immediately reverts back to action during the performance there is no shift in thinking there is only an immobilised mind caught up in what was wrong.

The trained brain will move to the missing step after not getting the result it needed and that missing step is:

DEALING WITH IT: Every elite performer in sports or business who has performed consistently has had this mindset. One that is prepared to deal with whatever the game or the situation throws at them and move from there in a constructive, creative manner. It is the ultimate in sports and, I believe, in life if in advance you make a commitment to deal with what the game throws at you, then success can be yours. You define it by what you become.

The current economic downturn is an example of using this philosophy. It becomes the mantra for peak performance in almost every situation you can imagine.

What is this here to teach me?

The question of what you have learnt is a good question when faced with the challenge ahead. The belief that there is something of value that the current conditions are here to teach and can help them act as a lesson is a good one to hold onto. The people we meet and the places we visit are the classroom to grow and develop in, in order to become even more than you are right now. Learning, quite rightly, is something which never stops.

Here is a thing to remember: When you *deal with* the challenge you loop back to what is possible. The questions then become:

Is it possible we could close the deal? Yes.

Do we definitely close the deal? No.

Do we definitely not close the deal? No

Is it possible we could close it though? Yes. That is the truth. It is that truth which leads to a state of mind that I hear clients describe when they are *in the zone,* when they are performing at their best. It is a state of calm that is the foundation for all peak performance. A 'knowingness' or certainty about themselves.

Now with this state of mind and commitment the next step is *clarity,* you need to 'know' what you want. Clarity of intention leads to that perfect picture in your mind. Every text on the Law of Attraction will have you focus on intention and the energy that you use in the mere thoughts about a certain person or goal you want to accomplish. The very act of prayer is intention and asking for what you want.

It is at this point that I will add the subtle change to the language because I am often asked about visualization. Some people cannot get that picture in their mind they struggle to 'see' the shot or movement or even scenario.

The subtle difference between visualization and

imagery is that imagery engages all the senses not just what you see internally or externally. You create the picture, notice if there are any sounds associated with the experience and you sense the feelings. With all this combined you are using imagery not just visualising.

After clarity of intention we are back to *action* again. The next step has to be that we need to do something. No matter how much intention you have the backside has to get out of the chair and when you take action, the more action you take the better you start to see *results*.

It is those results which are the guide to what will happen next. If the results are what you expected perfect. If, however, the situation doesn't turn out the way we expected then we have a choice. We loop back and question it or we develop a trained brain and learn to *deal with* it.

I don't care what application in sports, business or life you want to use this for but if you start to add this to your mental game you will find out how good you can be. There is no resistance to the challenge or the experience and you begin to welcome change.

The illusion of perfection

It is very easy sometimes to buy into the idea of perfection in sports or life. This is something which you need to resist. When the lesson of our time shows up we have to be able to look through lenses that have clarity and are not full of the noise of false perceptions (or worse, false ideals).

In 2005 I had one of those calls from the agent of Ryder Cup golfer and former World No 5 golfer Lee

Westwood. Lee was still looking to climb back up the world rankings after falling off the golfing radar. He had experienced a career high as No 5 in the world and is regarded as one of Europe's finest golfers. He has been outstanding in the Ryder Cup, just one of the most talented golfers Britain has produced, he is a winner who can sniff a victory a mile away.

It was the Monday of the Open Championship at St. Andrew's, the home of golf. I was looking forward to meeting Lee as I had been briefed that he had done almost no work on his mind, which because of his talent and success he wouldn't normally have been expected to have to, he had also dabbled with another coach and decided mental stuff wasn't for him.

He had become frustrated with his inconsistent performances and kept going back and asking poor questions mentally. When frustration creeps in that is a red light to a sportsman who is not enjoying what they do. I picked up that Lee wasn't hitting the shots he used to hit, he was being outplayed by players he had once outplayed and wanted to be back to 'putting it on a string' again.

The illusion of perfection often creeps in when a player is frustrated. It is a case that the expectations are much higher and they are not being met. I wanted to know about his best golf in 2000 when he won the order of merit title. After listening to him describe some of his best rounds and shots he was back there in the moment recalling vividly that year.

"Was your golf perfect that year? Did you hold the lead going into every final round? Did you find every fairway and green and two putt all day?" I asked knowing the answer.

He had a think about that great year and replied. "No. I was coming from back in the field a few shots behind. I was missing some fairways but scrambling well and getting up and down from all sorts of positions."

The long and short of it was that there was an "Illusion of Perfection". When he was at his very best he was prepared to deal with what the game threw at him. Leading, coming from behind to win it didn't matter to him. That was the mindset he had. This was a realisation he had to make before he could move on with his game. It has been great to see Lee back at his best and knocking at the door of the top players in the world again.

What illusions have you created in your own mind about perfection and how it has to be? I can guarantee that if you go back to the time when you have been unstoppable, those moments where you say. Yep, that was me! You will find that in those times you simply made a commitment to *deal with* what was thrown at you.

Your Notes:

Jamie Edwards

Chapter Seven

The Four Types

> *"Don't lower your expectations to meet your*
> *performance."*
> *-Sydney Smith*

Models are useful in some context because they allow you to follow and gauge where you are with your own game. This model is something that I use across sports and business alike. I use it because demystifying sports psychology is about removing any labels that have been associated with the word and which can act as a barrier. Whenever I ask a group I am presenting what images come to mind when they think of the word psychology usually they say things like:-

1.   Men in white coats
2.   Swinging watches
3.   Black leather couch
4.   Delve into the past
5.   Did you ride a pink bicycle when younger?

These are just some of the answers I get back from

them. The word psychology does frighten and has frightened people in the past. I have had many an elite athlete who has postponed or cancelled sessions because of the uncertainty of what will be involved in their sessions with me.

England flanker, Lewis Moody, once said "I saw it as a psychological weakness to have to speak with someone about my mental state."

After a recent speech I gave at a Microsoft event a businesswoman in the audience contacted me to speak with her about doing some work with her daughter. She had returned from the conference with enthusiasm to share with her seventeen year old daughter the idea of working on her mental game for middle distance running. Her daughter was very talented but was letting expectations get in the way of her progress. Unfortunately when she broached the idea of a performance coach or psychologist to her daughter, the girl's dismissive reply was "Mum, I'm not mad," or words to that effect.

So for something which has helped some of the best athletes and sportsmen and women in the world we really need to ask why all this resistance? My belief is that when a person can see how it applies to them then they can take action, the key is understanding what it can do for you.

Remember at school there were classes or subjects within those classes where you wondered where you would ever use the information you were learning? Remember algebra? Well, what follows is knowledge which you need in order to be able to assess how this is applicable to you. Apply the following to your world whilst making connections with the sporting world and fitting your models into the four types presented here:

1. UNTRAINED SKILLS: UNTRAINED BRAIN

This player is the player who hasn't much of an understanding of what needs to be done technically. Their skill development is basic and introductory and if they were to compete in a competitive situation they would be instantly challenged having to deal with anxiety or pressure or, usually, both. This is usually a beginner but not in all contexts.

2. TRAINED SKILLS: UNTRAINED BRAIN

This is a character you will be a little more familiar with. They usually have a word attached to them. That word is potential. How many times have you heard someone say: "He's got potential," about an athlete, a musician, a business person? Every day in my practice I hear a player tell me that he's been told that. Yet with the trained technical skills and talent (and in many cases I see in my working life a player or person who is not just technically skilled but have been blessed with an abundance of athletic talent) they still struggle to make headway. They usually practice better than they play. This person can perform in one environment and struggles to take their practice or training game to the real game. In golf they look good on the range. A good friend of mine told me last season he was 'playing great on the driving range' but couldn't transfer it to the golf course. I reminded him that although his passion for his improvement in the training environment was good to see it only matters if you can take it to the course.

In business this is the man or woman who knows everything about the product or service. They eat the manual for breakfast, lunch and dinner and yet if they go into the sales environment where they have to perform, they just don't seem to be able to get the job done. They have an untrained brain. The sales manager is forever saying to his director that they have potential but are just not fulfilling it. Think of two or three examples in a sport that you are familiar with.

Tim Henman would have been in this category because he was a textbook case. One of his coaches once told me that technically he was very good. Did he fulfil his potential? This is open to debate. He certainly got to certain points in matches and it wasn't about technique or ability that caused his undoing it was that elusive mental strength. Do you know of anyone close to you in this category?

3. UNTRAINED SKILLS: TRAINED BRAIN
Then we get to a character that I love dearly in sports, business and life because this person, this player doesn't have great technique. They have untrained skills. It doesn't mean that they never practice or apply themselves. It means that they are not 'textbook'. A golfer may have a quirky move in the swing, the tennis player likewise. The footballer would be the former legendary Arsenal and England centre-half Tony Adams. Tony, was not the most gifted or talented player but he had a great football brain. It was trained. The golfer doesn't look

impressive but you will be aware they have an ability to put the ball in the hole or get it round the course. Do you know the type? They are frustrating and they are in every walk of life because the chances are you are in this category too!

In business you find that this is the person in the office who has limited knowledge about the product or service yet they have a unique and uncanny way of making things happen. They connect with customers, have the communication skills to articulate their wants and can get things moving. They have a 'trained brain'.

Consider this for a moment. If you took category two and three over 100 matches, rounds, games, sales calls, whatever the performance number three would come out on top in over a 100 of them. On any given day the people who have trained skills but have an untrained brain will come out and blitz the person in three. They usually have to be in an environment they like or are comfortable with, playing with people they are comfortable with and (at the extreme end) have the moon in the correct position!

4. TRAINED SKILLS: TRAINED BRAIN

This is the player, person who has both trained skills and a trained brain. In modern sports you read about these people every day on the back pages of the newspapers, where the sports leader headlines are. Lewis Hamilton in his rookie season had the same car, technology as his teammate and still managed to take Formula One by storm. Why? Because he had developed a trained brain whilst at the same time worked on improving his driving skills.

Tiger Woods has trained both his skills and his brain from the age of 12 years old. His father Earl had the foresight to develop his son's mind at an early stage, to put the tools and concepts in place whilst he was young. To this day Tiger has probably not just the best mind in golf but one of the best minds in sport.

Federer is yet another example of someone who has trained his brain and whist he has enjoyed being the No 1 tennis player of this decade he hasn't always been in this category. There was a while when his mental skills were a long way from being the mental skills of a world No 1.

The conversation I had with a financial analyst brought home the difference in generations. He said his son had been introduced to mental training at work. He said that when he started in finance he had untrained skills but had a trained brain and an ability to learn and develop. There wasn't the technological sophistication we have today so he continued to rely on his ability to just make it happen.

Before his son's generation he said there was a generation of young people coming into finance who were very good technically but didn't have the skills to deal with the pressure. I found it interesting because he continued through his son to actually develop these skills with personal development and also with his own financial psychological development.

Which type are you? Your goal should be wherever you are in these four types to move on or have the intention as a player, coach, manager of a department or even someone just active in general life to work to get to stage four.

Your Notes:

Chapter Eight

Belief vs Trust

"If you don't know where you are going, any road will get you there."
-Lewis Carroll

What is the difference between belief and trust? Every player I have worked with in sports and every executive who has been off his game has had a bout of confidence loss. The problem with confidence loss is usually a loss of belief in ability. But many coaches will shout and stress in a pre-game talk that you have to believe in yourself. The signs are erected around the locker rooms or the office and they stress the importance of believing in yourself and the team.

In my own sporting background of playing basketball I often came up against players who believed in their ability. I spent two years at Archbishop Riordan High school in San Francisco, California where my mentor Alton Byrd plied his trade. It was a great opportunity for me to learn one of the skills of elite athletes, the ability to trust yourself in the heat of battle.

The way I was able to develop trust was to put myself in the situation over and over again but with a group of people who were going to stretch me beyond what I had ever experienced. You have to train yourself to trust your ability. The question is at what level do you train your skills? At 17 years old I left home to play more 'ball' . I didn't think I was getting enough basketball to be able to trust what I had developed. I wanted to train (which I did lots of as I was known as a gym rat), play against players who were leagues above my current ability and I wanted to test that training so San Francisco was the obvious place to go.

Whilst I developed my point guard skills, my leadership skills and my competitiveness went to an entirely new level. People in California were very competitive and if you walked down the street better than them they wanted to walk down the street better than you.

There was one lesson which I learned that stayed with me in sport and that I see in various sports as well as my work today: in 1859, Jean-Francois Blondin first completed one of the many death defying tightrope acts of his time by walking across the gorge below the Niagara Falls on a rope of more than 300m long and 50m above the water. His feat became that of legend and his fame and celebrity began to draw crowds of up to 5,000 people. Each trip across the water he would add more and more theatre to the stunt. A true entertainer who understood the concept of being a crowd pleaser he constantly developed his routine. "Who thinks I can walk this rope blindfolded?" he would ask the crowds that would gather.

"Yes, we believe you can do it." They would chant back. Off he would go to their amazement walking blindfolded across the gorge of the falls.

"Who thinks that I can take a wheelbarrow across?" he would ask.

"Yes, we have heard that you can do that too. We believe you." And so he would go off and again walk over the gorge to the amazement of the onlooking crowd.

And so he would continue with his performance by walking on stilts and sitting down midway while he cooked and ate an omelette. And I remember the first time I heard this story I was in total amazement that this man even lived and accomplished these feats.

Whist scanning the crowd he would ask "Who thinks that I can walk across the gorge with someone on my back? Who wants to come up here?" at this point as you can imagine the crowd started to look away quickly and shouted back "No! No! Not me."

The crowd believed in his ability to walk across the gorge as they had witnessed several times. Then out of the crowd came a voice, it was a young girl who said "I'll go with you."

The crowd responded angrily and said he shouldn't do it. They wouldn't let him carry out this stunt, only to be interrupted by the girl herself: "it's ok, he's my father. I trust him."

That would silence any protest.

That moment is also the lesson we all should take on board. There is a big difference between believing in your ability and trusting in it.

The little girl trusted her father's ability. When a peak performer has lost form, confidence and belief in themselves they have to reconnect to the unconscious part of them. The part of them that 'just knows' how to do something and goes ahead and does it with complete confidence in ability and without distractions and doubts.

Give me a call

One of the qualities we love about our friends is trust. We simply trust friends, that's why they are our friends. And so I refer to that other mind, the unconscious mind, as our friend. Your best friend even because in many situations you trust this friend to drive a car with another hunk of metal hurtling towards you on the other side of the road and you don't even question whether you are driving correctly. You trust 'your friend' to guide you. If you were to fall off your chair or stumble on the first step on the staircase your 'friend' puts your hand out to cushion the fall, just in time. We have heard many stories of human beings overcoming disease and becoming healthy by handing over their healing to their 'friend'. The inner power we all have on tap and which, however, gets utilised so infrequently.

So why do we become so disconnected from our 'friend'? We start to listen to that voice, the little voice that always wants to be heard. Think of the voice as the left side of the brain the analytical brain that calculates how long you have to get from one side of town to the other. It reminds you of when your dentist appointment is. It is also that voice that not only reminds you that you should be eating the chocolate but justifies it later. It is always questioning, being nosy as we say here in the UK, interfering.

So if you are to move from belief to trust letting go of that part of you that wants to interfere is the start. That part of you that interferes with trust needs to be stretched and needs evidence of having accomplished certain tasks.

It is very easy to stay the same. Get trapped in a role which endlessly repeats itself, a little like the lead hero in the film *Groundhog Day* but without the awareness that the day is endlessly repeating itself and therefore unable to do anything to change things.

Letting go = progress

Letting go of the past and the future does equal progress. Letting go of what you believed in because what you used to believe in can be limiting takes strength but it also tends to bring results. What we believed (notice my use of the past tense here) was in the past. The focus of attention for trust is in the present moment. Trust doesn't live in the future, trust doesn't live in the past. Trust is always experienced in the moment. And yet to get to trust, as I mentioned, you have to let go of the past, let go of what you have been currently doing and take on tasks which will stretch you beyond what you have ever experienced.

Swedish Vision for Business and Sports

Two golf coaches began to change the mindset for what was possible, initially, for Swedish golfers and later, as their work delivered results, further afield. They themselves are now regarded as being amongst the most innovative in the golf industry.

Pia Nilsson and Lynn Marriott came up with a concept known as Vision 54. They started to question why if the golfer has birdied a hole on a course, why can't they birdie every hole in that course. In fact, most players at some point at their home course have birdied every hole on their course. Especially if they can play a little.

If the par for the course was 72 then a birdie on every hole would represent 54. Most good players hold that elusive level par standard as being the holy grail of golf yet have birdied most if not all the holes on their course. So now you go out on the course with a new par...54!

On March 16th 2001 at Moon Valley country club, Phoenix Annika Sorentam played a historic round of golf shooting 59. A post round interview gave a clue into the mindset that she had adopted. The reporter, baffled at the historic performance had asked, "How did you do it?" almost as though a woman wasn't supposed to do such a thing.

Reflecting she added to the stock answers "…..I was still 5 over par!" The reporter was now bemused. Anniken had embraced the possibility that she could go out and shoot 54 and really this was all there was to it (at least on the surface, it is always a little more than just that).

What is your vision 54? Where in your life are you playing to par? Have you questioned the current limits that you place on your progress in sport, business and in life? It might be in education where students have stated they have a certain number of exams to pass with pre-determined grades. What is your Vision 54? Or it can be that the sales team that I worked with which had never broken the company best every month? Then with a shift in thinking that old record had been smashed based on two of the staff rewiring what was possible.

This is where you need to ask yourself: How can you raise your game and introduce Vision 54 to the organisation or your job?

Nothing ever gets better if you don't question current practice.

Your Notes:

Chapter Nine

Shelve it

"Man should forget his anger before he lies down to sleep."
-Mohandas Karamchand Gandhi

Finding a place to put your thoughts in and organise them is a challenge. If they are not shelved they end up playing in your head over and over again. That's the loop of insanity I discussed earlier. When you can shelve them, organise them and create a place for them so you can go to work on your mental state you undertake a process known as awareness. Your mental Ketchup should be easy to get to, always at hand.

Most coaching and training focuses on what you do during the activity. If you are a telesales executive you will be coached what to say *during* the call. If you look at the four shelves which follow, you will find that your mental game in your life and business will fit into one of them.

SHELF 1 - BEFORE: How you think before you walk into a meeting, the thoughts you have will have an impact on what you say during the meting. The thoughts that an athlete has before the competition will have an impact on his or her performance. It is no different from you in the office or the context that you perform in almost every other sphere of activity. The thoughts like "Oh no, I have to meet the CEO, or I am playing against this player and the last time I played against them they ate my lunch. Other thoughts such as "it's raining and I never play well in the rain." Which is a common excuse for the amateur golfer. All of these have an impact. Thoughts which are negative and excuse driven, generally, tend to provide excuses for failure.

SHELF 2 - DURING: What you do during the activity, the rituals and the mindset during the activity is where most training in the corporate world and sports coaching is geared to. If you are going to go to the next level this is the area you need to spend the least amount of time in because you have spent plenty of time here before.

SHELF 3 - IN BETWEEN: The in-between phase is one of the most overlooked aspects of the mind, depending on the context where you are you will find that the time spent in the DURING or IN-BETWEEN phase can be disproportionate for different sports. The in-between in Golf can be as much as 85% of not playing the sport, which means it involves doing something other than playing golf. Only 15% of the time you are playing golf. In tennis depending on the surface you can expect it to be an approximately 60:40 split between during and in-between.

The real skill in sports and life is the ability to switch off. Not switch on because we all have that ability to concentrate and focus when the time requires it. Athletes are often told to concentrate by coaches and kids are asked to concentrate by parents and teachers. Whenever I ask those coaches and parents "Did you ever have a lesson in concentration when younger?" The answer is normally no.

"So why, if you have never had a lesson yourself do you ask others to concentrate?" I usually ask. That doesn't make sense. Yet the ability to recover, to replenish, to switch on and more importantly off is a skill in itself. Burnout is definitely a challenge for executives, it's a challenge for sportsmen and women. Later you will find some tools to help you switch off whether that is at the end of the day after work or if you want to develop your skills in the sporting arena, at the end of a demanding match when you need to be able to replenish your mental resources.

SHELF 4 - AFTER: This one is the silent assassin of the mind. Probably one of the more important places you can look at and which is often overlooked. This shelf explores how you review and process what you do. How do you process the meeting you have just attended? How do you process the performance? How do you process the winning performance and the losing performance? The mind needs feedback if it is to function properly in its assessment and there are one or two ideas that you should incorporate into your world in order to add another dimension to your game.

Your Notes:

Jamie Edwards

Chapter Ten

The art of state control

"Courage is the discovery that you may not win, and trying when you know you can lose."
-*Tom Krause*

When you go to a meeting, to a training session or you are getting ready to perform some complex action you will find yourself in a certain frame of mind or in a certain state of being. Depending on past results your state can be affected by many other factors. Think of a striker in football if he is in a poor run of form. His confidence is low and his team mates are waiting for the goal to come. They are waiting for the good shot, the great performance to feel good.

In a situation like this it is like having a weight on your shoulders carrying the baggage of under performing. The flip side of "waiting is weighting" is that if you don't hit the good shot or if the good performance eludes you then you feel bad and this affects your game. Being in the right state to perform is key to success and this includes being able to deal with and neutralise the weight of expectation.

Exercise

Now, take a pen and paper and draw a triangle. At the top of the triangle put the word STATE, at the bottom left of the triangle put the word DECISIONS and at the bottom right of the triangle put in the word TECHNIQUE. This is the trained brain 'poor shot' triangle. It was developed working with golfers who consistently blamed their technique for their poor shots and would get angry and frustrated when they had worked on their skills in practice and couldn't transfer their learning to the real game.

Keep in mind there are only three ways to hit a poor shot:

1.Decision: You made a poor decision or the wrong decision.

2.Technique: The incorrect technical move was executed.

3. State: You were in the wrong state of mind for the task at hand.

It is worth remembering here that while decision making and technique will have an impact on scores and performances in most activities, we cannot escape the fact our mental state affects our decision making process. If you are in a good mood you make better decisions in that mood than you will if you are in a lousy mood or a poor state of mind.

State has an impact on both **Decision** and **Technique** so it is important for you to understand what creates your states and more importantly the states in others.

The 15:20 Rule

Before or during any performance in sports or business I coach the 15/20 rule. This rule is simple. It creates an awareness of state when the autopilot kicks in and starts with probing questions. If you check the state you are in at a given moment or the present moment and rewind 15 or 20 minutes beforehand you will find the cause of the present feelings. Depending on the sport or the context it could be a 5-10 minute rule. I was working with an aspiring golfer recently who had a problem with putting well on the 18th hole. This was on any course not just at his home course!

There is a well-documented if somewhat anecdotal phenomenon known as a bogey hole where you have a negative emotional attachment to a specific hole on a golf course. This is created when a mistake is made and instead of reducing emotion the exact opposite happens and the player 'blows up' (for anyone who has not seen the Kevin Costner movie *Tin Cup* which perfectly illustrates the 'blow up' principle, I need to stress again the sensitivity of golf and emotional content). At the cellular level the mind records this differently than a normal event because there has been increased emotion. Think of a favourite song. What or whom does it remind you of? A wedding, an old flame or even a holiday destination or a significant time of your life. Well that same process is happening in your own mind concerning specific places or specific events or specific sequence of events.

So back to the aspiring golf professional. I told him about the 15/20 rule and that his anxiety on the green starts before he even steps on it. We had been working for months on staying present, keeping in to the moment. Keeping his monkey mind in check as it was prone to jump ahead a few holes as he came down the stretch and jump back into the past agonising over a mistake he had just made, probably due to the fact that he was not concentrating on the present.

"The anxiety isn't triggered by the 18th. You have associated that feeling with being on the last green. Let's go back 5 minutes before." He looked puzzled and rewound his thoughts to the approach shot to the green. "Play the shot in your mind and then listen to your commentary after you have seen the result." I continued, "what did you say?"

"I *need* to hole this!" he declared.

"How far back from the green are you when you make this statement?"

"150 yards," he added knowing that he has allowed his mind to jump forward before even walking on the green. "You are saying that this statement has created the anxiety long before I have stepped onto the putting surface?"

"The emotions that we all feel in sports or life can be traced back 15 minutes before. Those thoughts prior to the actions contribute to what we are feeling in the moment."

Do mental states spread? Yes they do. We all know people who light us up when we are in their presence. If you are having a day where you are not feeling your best this can affect those around you. The reality is that these days do occur. If you are feeling confident this can also affect those around you. In times of personal and professional controversy how you feel will have a direct impact on your team. It is important to self check your own state before engaging in activity or dialogue with others.

The Happ-O-Meter

One of the most effective uses of state management was in 2004 when a group of senior managers and MD's attended a trained brain networking event in Greater Manchester. When it came to the topic of the Art of State Control a businessman named Charles told a story about his P.A. knowing what type of day it was going to be based on how he walked across the car park and into the office. She had been fed up with the Jekyll and Hyde personality that her boss had displayed on several occasions. Sitting him down in her office one day she read him her riot act.

"I know exactly what type of day this company's going to have based on what mood you come into this office," she said quite sternly to her boss. "If you're in a bad mood, the whole place is in a bad mood, it spreads, if you walk across that car park in a good mood I can tell what type of day we are going to have. I am going to start marking you out of ten every day. 10 is good 1 is real bad. Starting tomorrow morning."

Next morning Charles said he was adamant that he was going to score well on his PA's 'Happ-O-Meter'. He walked across the car park with his head up and his shoulders back with a very big smile on his face. He walked through the door and she said, "Seven!" He was happy with a seven, but being the competitive businessman he was he wanted to beat it the following morning. Again, with his newfound awareness of his state of mind and the realisation that it was having an impact on his staff he got out of his car and strode into the office.

"Six!" Shirley, said as he looked for approval. What was interesting as Charles relayed it to the group after we had brought up the topic of controlling the state of mind internally was that he had more awareness of his mood swings rather than floating through the day on auto pilot, going in and out of negative states and occasionally the odd positive one. Awareness is everything and it is something which you can cultivate.

The Art of State Control

1. Understanding: What creates your state of mind? Do you know what is going on within your body and mind to create your moods?

2. Awareness: Do you know you are in that state?

3. Alteration: Can you alter and change your state of mind yourself rather than expecting the outside world to do it for you? There is no sense waiting for something to happen to you.

4. Utilisation: Where can you use this winning state of mind in the appropriate context? Example of that would be in sport such as golf. You might have the state of calm as a tool. Some players may want to be calm before holing a sliding left to right 6ft putt and yet smash a 300 yard drive they may require a more determined state that wouldn't be useful on the greens.

With a lack of understanding of the factors that make up and contribute to an athlete or person having control of their state of mind, they sentence themselves to a lifetime of frustration and poor performance. The key components of state control are the movie mind and how one uses their physical body as a tool to achieve certain things. Upon this note it's time to explore the mind as a movie.

The DVD Menu

In his book the *Movie Mind*, Michael Hall refers to the concept as viewing our thoughts as cinematic experiences. Each emotion that we experience day to day, in the workplace as well as in sport has a corresponding movie that is playing behind it. This movie that is playing can be of a time when one has been more confident. That specific time would be the 'confidence' movie. You may have had a time when you are anxious, concerned about the future. The emotion is a manifestation of the unconscious movie that is playing on the screen of the mind. The movie may be of an event or some decision in the future, something that is occupying your thoughts but the feelings are experienced in the present moment.

The opposite also applies to the feelings of frustration, anger or disappointment. Primarily these emotions are attached to the past. The movies that are associated with the past or said differently the memory of the past will bring about feelings in the present which will have an impact upon the present.

Key point: Consider carefully what movies you are playing each and every day. This is about becoming aware of the movies that are running, that are creating the states that you experience daily, when you are performing. If you watch a DVD you are presented with options *before* you press play. Those options determine which scene of the movie you will watch. You can literally skip all the boring parts and go directly to your favourite part of the film; therefore missing out anything which is not as exciting.

If you could step out of this experience and sit yourself in the theatre, sit in a seat where you have a good view of this experience; it is literally like watching yourself on the screen.

Now do this: think of your three favourite films of all time and jot them down so you can see them in front of you. As you think of those films, what emotions do they create? How do you feel just recalling those images?

Imagine inside your mind you have a screen or a plasma TV and your thoughts are a collection of movies. What you play on the screen will make you feel something. Behind *all* the emotions there is a movie playing. If you put a horror film on you will experience fear, a comedy will make you laugh, you'll connect with intense feelings watching a romantic love story. What goes on, on the screen will make you feel something. Sports are a collection of movies that have been stored and can be replayed. Helping an athlete to perform at their best means watching the blockbusters and avoiding the flops.

Before training, *before* the start of an event my players have access to three movies so that they can choose which state of mind is needed for that event. This is like having a DVD menu to choose from.

On the Scale

Consider carefully, on a scale of 1 to 10 where do you
need to be to perform at your best? One would be like
relaxing on a beach in the Maldives and ten would be
like going 12 rounds with Mike Tyson. Where would
you say you had to be to perform at your best? As you
think about that ask yourself what is the state of mind
that will help you access close to the number which
best reflects the sate of mind you need?

What Moody?

Leicester Tigers and England No 7, Lewis Moody had
just come off one of the lowest points in his career.
Never in 100 years of Rugby had an England player
been sent off at Twickenham. It was one of the lows
of his career. One of his sponsors Red Bull who were
also a client of Trained Brain had suggested that he
meet with me. It took a while, a couple of months
before we could overcome all the natural hesitancies
and he sat down for his first session.

He later went on to say "I was really sceptical at
first. I always thought seeing someone was a sign of
mental weakness. Jamie made such a big difference,
it's been amazing."

He mentioned being sent off on more than one
occasion and it was beginning to become a pattern. I
asked him on a scale of 1 to 10 where would he have
to be in order to be at his very best. He replied with
an eight or a nine measure. At this point, when your
nickname is 'Crazy Horse' or 'Mad Dog' and you have
a history of being sent off and you put your body on

the line like Lewis has done throughout his career for both club and country, I wasn't going to buy into that straight away.

As a coach my job is not to accept the filtered response and to dig a little deeper. I asked him so I could confirm his belief and he said yes. I got myself pumped up first.

"Tell me a bout you best rugby. Can you remember a specific time when you have been at your very best?" I asked.

"Yeah, it was at Welford Road against Newcastle."

I asked him to go back to the time he was getting ready *before* the match. "Notice what you can see, hear and feel about that match," I continued. He was looking up at the ceiling almost searching for the answers up there but actually accessing a part of his mind that stores images.

"Go back to *before* the match. What were you like before that match?"

"Calm, I was calm." He said with a tone of surprise in his voice. "About a three or four."

It is very revealing when you find out that what you have been doing and what you did when at your best. Lewis recognised that calm was the foundation of his peak performances. Calm is a common thread in peak performance in sports business and life. As the base emotion all other emotions can be built on top of calm.

Which Movie?

When you feel stressed at work will you play the *The Stressed Movie* or you'll play *The Happy Movie, The*

Anger Movie or *The Relaxed Movie*. Confidence has a movie; when you feel anxious or nervous you have to play a certain movie. The real skill of the mental game is to become aware of your habitual movies not just react to them as most of them are unconscious. So what really should you do in order to achieve that? Let's go and see.

Create the Menu

1. Think of three states of minds that you want to have access to throughout the day. Choose what state you want to be in before you start. Do you want to be confident, calm, courageous, focused, determined or playful?

2. Now match the movie for the state of mind you want to access. In other words go back to a particular time when you have been, for example, confident. Notice the sensory details what you could see, hear, and feel. Notice what sounds you hear, what words are being used, what do you say to yourself, how did you move, breath, stand when you were confident and at your best?

3. Repeat this for the other two.

Who has your PIN number?

Too often we allow ourselves to be drained mentally, emotionally, physically by not taking the necessary steps to ensure that we are ready to deal with what the game of life will throw at us. We saw in my introduction the explanation that everyone has two bank accounts.

A wealthy American once said to me "Jamie, there are two bank accounts in life. A Financial bank account and an Emotional bank account." And continued "as low as most people's financial accounts are, their emotional bank account is even lower."

If you are going to deal with the game and what it throws at you then you need some reserves in your account. If you give people such as your boss, the manager, your friends, partners or your children the PIN number to your account then they will just drain it. Everytime you need some emotional cash you find you are in the red. You wouldn't give your cash PIN number to just anyone. Why do you give your emotional PIN number out to people you don't even know or if you do know them let them drain your resources with negativity? If you are to let people have access to it make sure they are helping you to fill it with emotional currency you can use rather than drain it so that you do not have the reserves you need when you need them.

Deposits in your bank book

One of the best ways to deposit into that emotional bank account is to keep a journal. For many years writing has been one of the best ways to capture the memories of a day or a week. Memoirs of the rich and famous have been fascinating the world and giving us an insight into how they think. Martina Navratilova said that she really took her Tennis to the next level when she started to write down what she did well based on the advice of a Hollywood legend. Many business leaders have a journal for their most creative ideas that can be recorded the moment they pop up into their consciousness.

The Bank Book is used to write down the three best or most memorable events of your day. In sports I call it, depending on the sport of course, a Shot diary. I have the athlete write down the three best shots, tackles if they are a midfielder, catches or best moments of their event. In sports the slump is something that can put any player on a path that they don't like going down mentally and may find it tough to get back on track. Keeping a record of the small things that you do well by writing them down is a way that allows you to recall the details of the experience and create a moment which has a lasting impact on your career and your life.

Sensory rich is the key phrase here. Jotting down how you felt, what you saw, noticing what sounds were associated with the moment and what was not. How did you stand, walk, breathe? The more details the deeper you burn the DVD in your mind to be recalled again and the larger the deposit in the account.

In any game or situation you can always find something good or constructive that happened if you look deep enough. You want to avoid writing about what didn't work. This isn't about getting it out of your head. That is a different style of journalling altogether and is useful in a different context, so right now we need to focus on all the things which have worked.

The aim is to create a book that you can flick

through full of deposits. Imagine that you have been keeping a shot diary or bank book for two weeks. Will that change how you think? Not really. But take yourself four weeks out and beyond and you keep writing down what happened that day, what you did in training, in a game or more importantly in life and you will have created some new pathways in your mind. A new habit of how to process your events of that day.

Stop the 'If Only'

Unfortunately misery loves company. Which is why the media thrives on negative stories. It is why the clubhouse in sports or the bar are full of stories of "if only". If only I had done this, if only I had not missed that shot, if only the referee had seen the handball. Life is full of 'if only' moments. Going back into the past and replying 'if only' makes for a frustrated and disappointed experience in the *after* quadrant.

Ben Crenshaw, one of the greatest putters in the history of golf was given the best advice from his mentor Harvey Penick once. "Ben, only go to dinner with good putters."

That statement indicates that the talk over dinner will be of successful putts not which ones were missed and this tends to create an uplifting, energising, instructive atmosphere which helps everybody.

Who you go to dinner with and how do you process your day are intertwined and create a positive feedback in your mind. Now don't mistake this for "airy fairy nothing, bad ever happens" type of thinking. Of course your days and mine can be thrown into a spin with events that we have no control of. Writing down the three best events or shots does by no means change a bad day into a good one. It does however put closure on the day. On a great day it enhances the day as in order to recall and write down what is going on you have to replay the event on your mental screen which means that it can, if necessary, become part of your 'DVD' menu.

If you are going about your business every day and you don't play sports then simply write down what happened at work, on the way, how the kids made you smile or just thinking of them or some act of kindness that you experienced.

The mind loves to be rewarded. The law of reward states that if you stop giving your mind pleasure then it will stop moving towards it. We are hardwired to avoid pain. Take all the moments and experiences in your day for granted and your mind will stop focusing on simple pleasures.

Think of it like this. We are so used to looking for what is wrong in life. If you look for what is wrong you tend to find it. This is why it is so important to be able to control your thoughts and thinking.

The Race Book

Downhill Mountainbike Team, Atherton Racing have had success using this very tool. Rachel, the youngest of the three siblings had broken her wrist in what was a pivotal part of the 2007 season. The World Championships were to be held on home soil at Fort William and one of Rachel's goals was to become World Champion. As the unconscious mind needs evidence and not fiction I asked her to write down the good points after her practice runs and also after her race runs. She started to collate a detailed list of what she was doing well. Like the TV chefs who have recipe books, Rachel had started to identify some of the ingredients that contributed to her success. This meant that each week she only had to repeat what she was doing. This was a new insight for her. Then her season was thrown into a spiral as she came off her bike in practice and broke her wrist. My first call to her was to offer my commiseration. Then when she had settled down and the event had sunk in it was time to get to work on her resolve. She was feeling sorry for herself and I said that her recovery would be hindered in the state of mind she was currently in.

For the next seven days I asked her to read her race book. As part of her daily routine she trained physically and she had a couple of mental exercises to do one of which was to re-read the whole of her book.

"It's really keeping me in a good place. I keep reading certain races where I have competed well and the whole event comes back to me. I feel much better," she told me during a session.

After nearly two months of rehab on her wrist, staying in great shape and competing in her mind every day combined with reading all of her Bank Book she returned to Fort William and picked up the silver medal finishing second. A career high finish up to that point in a major championship.

Rachel had embraced the practice of journalling her thoughts and the events of the day and had no idea that something as simple as that would have such an impact. She said it was great because her mind was going back to the times, races and situations she had written about and it gave her the proof that she could ride and not to let doubt creep in and undermine her ability.

Evidence. The minds needs evidence that it can do something. Belief is created with small steps of evidence and the ingredients to make it happen again and again. Not telling yourself that you can do it. That is pumping yourself up, but knowing that you can do it and having the facts to back it up.

Erabu Thinking

The Japanese word for choice is Erabu. To choose is one of the greatest assets of being human or should I say a human being. The animal kingdom doesn't have the same capacity as we do to choose our thoughts and so with the evolutionary advantage over the many other species on the planet we can literally think whatever we want.

The problem with choice is if we have trained ourselves to think of what we don't want it becomes really hard to think of what we do want. The DVD menu combined with the Bank Book are perfect tools for focusing your attention on what you do want and what you have done well.

On your movie screen in your mind 'Think of the colour of your front door.' Did you bring up the image on the screen? In that instance you could have chosen differently. You could have brought to mind the neighbour's front door or your back door. This is exactly what is meant by Erabu: To choose. Now if you are choosing to watch the horror films in your life, then you are indulging in the connection to the horror films which suddenly makes you responsible for the movie list and associated negative energy (and emotions) of your horror movies.

The Poor Shot Triangle

In sports there are only three ways to perform poorly. Often players will look at me with surprise thinking how can that possibly be true. But when you look at it closely and follow the example below you will relate to this both in and out of the sporting arena.

1. DECISION making which affects performance.
2. TECHNIQUE which breaks down on the day.
3. STATE of mind not being where you want it to be.

Look at the triangle. There are days when your technique, may be in very good shape and you are 'feeling it' on this day but your decision making isn't quite right. There are many factors that can influence decision making but no matter how good your technique is on that occasion if you are simply making poor decisions it will affect your performance or outcome for the day. Likewise, the decision making can be very good. You choose the correct stroke, shot or words to say but when you come to execute the action your technique lets you down.

Finally, lets, look at 'state'. If you are in the wrong state of mind does that affect your decision making? If you are in a bad mood do you tend to make bad decisions? When people, especially athletes are in a good mood they tend to make good decisions. The waiting really is weighting. Often sportsmen and women who are off target are waiting for their performances to hit them in the face again. They are waiting for the goals, the putts to roll in. In business you are waiting or hoping that the deals will come in or they will say yes to your proposal. If it does you feel good, likewise if it doesn't you feel bad. That's' the flip side of any performance and isn't just restricted to sports, it sweeps right across the board of almost every human activity.

The Hungry Mind

The 'hungry mind' is not the Polly Anna of positive thinking "I'm happy, I'm happy, I'm happy" when your whole world is falling apart. There is a lot of reality that has to be added. However, the mind wants to hang on to a past that doesn't serve you. In fact it wants to feed off it. The mind gets very hungry. It wants to be fed all of the time. It's fuel is energy. Any type of energy, and depending on what type of energy you have been feeding it or what has become the norm it will crave more and more of it.

Negative energy becomes like a drug. Like food it can be addictive and the mind wants to indulge in overeating or overfeeding. The paradox of the negative energy is the feeding of positive energy which comes from thought.

So in your professional life the food for thought is 'Feel Good First, Perform Second'.

Think of a recent time where you have had a task or job to complete and you have been 'waiting to feel good'.

The tip of the triangle is 'state' and state has an impact on both decisions and technique. So it is more important to learn what creates your state of mind as it affects the other two parts of the triangle.

The Movie Trailer: Glimpse Multiplication

Whenever you have a flash of brilliance, you see what you could do and you cannot get it back but it comes in flashes I call it glimpse multiplication. Sometimes you see yourself doing what you want, you get a sense of what is possible and sometimes that voice in your head tells you that there is a way and you are close or even that you have it. It is that very second or instant and for some it is an instant and for others it is moments and for others it can be days or weeks. Depending upon where you put yourself in that category these glimpses of brilliance can be fleeting or last a while but they are glimpses that often spark questions of "why can't I do that more often?, Why can't I do it everyday? I know I can do it." What usually follows glimpse multiplication is frustration. This emotion is based on not feeling fulfilled. That potential hasn't been reached.

The way to make it last is to keep playing the movie. Keep playing the glimpse that is flashing on the screen. The amount of times that I hear that someone has neglected to replay an event or memory that makes them feel great would have been enough for me to become a millionaire.

Take the mind being like a movie as we have discussed and then the glimpses are like trailers to the movie. When you go to the movie theatre you are always presented with a trailer before the feature film. This trailer tends to be a preview of the up and coming releases and there is, usually, a variety of them. All of which have different ratings. Your mind is exactly the same. It is always flashing across the screen a number of trailers. These are glimpses of an emotion. A trailer about the argument you just had with your boss. A trailer about the worry of being made redundant and the potential consequences of that. This trailer is playing out in the mind with full surround sound and is in High definition.

The glimpse could be of a sporting event that you are going to play in the future and have created enough anxiety about the outcome.

The real question here is what do you do with the trailers? Awareness is just the start of the process. When you become aware of the negative trailer or its glimpses you can influence your own mind. Notice how the trailer is being presented to you. Visually do you see the movie or is it something that you hear first? Or it may be something that you get a feeling for first? Let's examine what techniques we can apply which can help us.

The Breath: *Mushin* is the Japanese word for 'no mind' or mindfulness. *Mushin* is the first step to slowing down the trailers.

Put your attention on your breathing now. Notice the rise and fall of your breathing. Put your attention on the breath and just notice it. Be aware of your breath. When your attention is on the breath the trailer slows right down the mind stops racing. The paradox to the negative trailer is noticing the trailers that make you feel good. These trailers are the ones that often go unnoticed because the mind has been fed with negative glimpses of past events. There tends to be a feedback loop here which allows negative glimpses to reinforce negative glimpses and affect performance, but the same can be applied to positive ones.

Trailer v Highlight Film

Producing your own trailer or highlight film couldn't be easier. Now with today's technology you can do this with the latest home filmmaking kits but this is the way to enhance your experiences not supplant the written method. When you write something down it has a way of burning your own DVD much deeper than just watching something on a computer or a television screen. The act of writing means you replay the movie in your own mind in great detail. You have to think about the event and then record it yourself at a cellular level.

The addition of your real event being captured on film will enhance your movie mind.

Trailers are usually of one event with flashes of that event and different stages. Just like if you were seeing the shortened exciting parts of the latest Hollywood blockbuster that was to be released.

The Highlight differs because this can be of several events from different contexts that make up the film. The highlights can be from different timescales. You may have played your sports for several years and want to create a highlight film over your career. It may be of a season that you had.

It may even be a review of the year. Do this once and you have it forever in your mental archives:

1. Pick an event or situation that you often take part in.
2. Think of several situations which have resulted in good results for you. If you have had great results add those to them.
3. Write a list of headings.

Here are some examples to get you started but feel free to write your own:

Sales pitch for new product in March.

Meeting with the director last month.

Handling of office conflict.

Contract Signed.

Bonus Day!

Now you have a put together some highlights you can use. Go back to each heading and write down a very brief description of that experience in sensory rich detail. For example, *BONUS DAY: Walked into office and picked up cheque*. This is a start but it is not a good sensory-rich example.

A much better one would be: *I walked across to the other building where my bosses office is located full of anticipation. She had congratulated the team on the mammoth volume of sales we generated, a personal best for me and my team. All I could see was the new car I was going to buy, I had this big grin on my face but had to compose myself as I got to the door. The butterflies in my stomach were getting stronger as she handed me a cheque with that amount on. PAYEE: Francis Green. That's all I could see. My first big bonus cheque!*

That is an example. The richer the better. The easier it is going to be to put the clips together. Now repeat for each heading that you have.

Sports events would work exactly the same way.

Create the heading first. They do not have to be winning events, it can be part of an event or game. It can be a glimpse of brilliance or a spell. You are the director of the film. You decide what is going to make up this highlight film for you.

Next step is to read and connect all the events, experience all the events again one after the other. This floods your mind with positive impact emotionally or PIE as I call it (acronyms are useful as they make us remember things and, as in this case, also raise a smile). Once you have had your PIE then you read what you have written again three or four times. Make sure you are sat up or stood up when you do this.

Breakfast, lunch and Dinner

For the next seven days, you should recall your highlight film for breakfast, lunch and dinner. You would never miss all of those meals in a day would you? I hope not. If you missed breakfast you wouldn't miss lunch or dinner so if you miss your breakfast highlight you repeat at lunch and dinner.

Then just add music: You can enhance the highlight of a film by adding music, your favourite music to this and as they say in Hollywood 'Score'the film. Depending on what type of highlight film you have put together will depend on the music.

Read the scripts again, go back and experience those times and flood your mind and body with the experience again and again. You can crank up the feelings or reduce them by imagining you have a volume button that could control what and how you listened to any sounds associated with that day.

Turn the volume up and you will find the feeling changes and turn it down and the feeling can change again. Listening to music whilst you are in this peak state will add more to the experience. Why do athletes listen to music when they are on the way to the game or even just before the performance? They have created a link or an association to that music. It becomes their pre-game tune. If they don't listen to it they feel something is missing from the ritual and they do not feel right in themselves.

Rocket Man

During the Ashes series in 2005, I asked Freddie did he like music. He said yes and reeled off a number of artists, one of who was Elton John. I asked him who had control of the CD player in the dressing room. There is always someone who is the team DJ. It was normally him but in that instant because of the out of ordinary state of mind he was in during the start of the series he had not paid any attention to music and that role of leadership by example and connecting with teammates.

I said that it would be a good idea that he took charge of the music in the dressing room and played the music that he liked. Which he went away and did. After that series victory, Elton John sent the team a crate of Champagne to congratulate them after hearing that his hit 'Rocket Man' had become the theme of the series. If that Ashes winning team was to hear that tune again it would take them back to those winning times during that historic victory.

For the next level we will need to move on from just listening to music to scoring the movie so that you don't even need to have the actual music to hand because it will be *embedded* in your memory.

If you are married you will have a wedding song that you danced to. If that music came on now you would experience the feelings of that day and more than likely the images, emotions and the highlights of that day would come flooding back. In this instance the images are embedded into the music. It is like a song that may remind you of a holiday, or a certain person that you dated.

They trigger the memories. The ones you want to remember and the ones you want or would like to forget. When people ask me about motivation I ask them what is the movie that they are playing on their mental screen? When you put together your trailer or highlight film you will have the initial push to access the state of mind that you get to when you are really motivated. There are times when you don't question it. You just put your shoes on, don your kit and go. The times you question that and you think about sitting down when you get home, putting the TV on or lying on the bed because of exhaustion you tend to be communicating in ways that support that. Use your films.

How does it feel to be in flow?

Your Notes:

Jamie Edwards

Chapter Eleven

The Mont Blanc Mindset

"Stop trying to fit in when you were born to stand out."
- Movie: What a Girl Wants

In an early chapter I referred to Mont Blanc. What type of pen are you? How do you write your story, your history? How you go about documenting, producing the story of your life, your career or professional life?

The Mont Blanc mindset isn't about how much you are worth. It's not about looking down at the person with the Bic pen. It is a mindset. My Uniball writes better than my Mont Blanc. But that reminds me it's a symbol of perceived value and that all pens do the same job.

What do Trump, Beckham, Apple, Harley Davidson, Nike, Oprah and Mont Blanc all have in common? They are all brands that have a value to their clients or customers. Their value isn't based on what they do. It is based on who they are just as the Mont Blanc has value because of its brand rather than the sheer quality of its writing.

What do I mean? If Donald Trump puts his name

on anything its value quadruples because of who he is. Take two buildings standing side by side. It costs the same to build them both but if you add the Trump name to one, its value would soar above the other. When David Beckham puts his name to something it sells out. When Apple produces a new product it out-sells its rivals. This is because many of our favourite brands have a perceived value to us. You are emotionally attached to certain products or services. As a result, leaving that brand relationship to use a competitor is highly unlikely because of that emotional bond. We all have a brand that we love, but you need to ask yourself this question: do your clients feel the same about you and your service? Start thinking like a brand was advice that a mentor once mentioned to me.

Married to a brand

All brands have equity, like property they have values that rise and fall. Personal branding is something dependent on culture and the part of the world you are in. As a result brand promotion (or the lack of it) can be seen as self-promotion, arrogance, lack of confidence in your service or playing small because it will offend someone.

We know the difference is not always what you know, but who you know, and not what you say but how you say it. Speaking to a group of golf professionals in Oxford, UK I emphasized that the challenge for them was to stop thinking of themselves being in the coaching business and start thinking about being in the business of marketing their coaching business.

Developing your brand equity

Brands all have equity, yet personal branding or marketing in the UK is not promoted like it is in the US, even though we know the difference is not always what you know, but *who* you know, and not what you say, but *how* you say it.

A former tabloid editor had interviewed two British Actors in Hollywood and asked them about the differences between the UK and the USA. Both were quick to reply that the British mentality was to play down your achievements for not wanting to sound like you are bragging. "It was just a small film," she continued by adding her belief that if you cannot talk about your own success who will, and that in Hollywood you have to be comfortable with that. What can you learn and how can you apply it to your life?

I call it the The Oprah Effect. The US media mogul is world class at promoting others and is not too bad either at communicating what she is good at and what she believes in.

What do you believe in? Are you comfortable with communicating that what you do, promote, sell, contribute to? Or do you play the "Small Game"? Is it time for you to stand out or just add even more value to your own brand?

Here are the guidelines you need for you to develop your brand equity. This is a valuable exercise.

1. List two to four products, events or services you are known for. Now list one or two additional items you plan to be known for by this time next year.
2. List one to three ways in which your current job or project is challenging you.
3. List one to three new facts you have learnt in the last 90 days.
4. Your Visibility Branding Programme: list two to four ways in which you are visible locally, regionally and nationally if it applies to what you do.
5. List two to three names you have added to your address book in the last 90 days. People who are or could be influential in your life or career. These can be from within the industry or outside of the industry you work in.
6. What activities are you going to undertake over the next 60-90 days that will enhance your CV?
7. List three ways in which your CV - Profile today is different from this time last year.

By making these lists you will have a better understanding of where you stand as a brand, and how you can improve as a brand. It is important to realise that in order to be a brand that stands out, to attract business and retain customers, you need to take on relevant projects and challenges, and achieve them.

Questions are the Answer

Just like playing sports, what you focus on in business has an impact on your state of mind. Create a habit of asking yourself what will you be doing to improve your CV over the next 60 - 90 days?

"I don't want to go right," or "Don't miss it on the

left" are the on-course equivalents of walking into the supermarket with a list of everything you *don't* want. Imagine what your actions would be like with a shopping list of what you *don't* want: quite erratic, walking up and down aisles you don't need to be in.

Get into the habit of asking yourself what you want. The brain needs clarity even for the smallest tasks. It craves clarity of intention.

The traffic lights test

To take your performances to the next level there are some more questions you need to ask yourself, and you need to come up with the answers. I have my personal clients ask themselves these questions every month. Draw yourself a set of lights and then write the following questions:

RED: What do I or we need to STOP doing that is not making me or us, if it's a team, successful?

AMBER: What do I/we need to KEEP doing; that makes me/us successful?

GREEN: What do I/we need to START doing; that will make me/us more successful next year?

Fifty percent of what you know doesn't determine how good you will be. If you take a group of hairdressers or even doctors. What makes a good hairdresser? It is the way they cut hair. The skill, because most hairdressers have the skill. Does a GP have the same technical skills that the GP in the next room has? Yes they do. But what separates the GP? It's the other 50%. What separates the hairdresser? The other 50%. The skill of influence, the personal marketing skills, the communication skills. Knowing how to make the connection with your clients and ultimately make them feel at ease.

What is the other 50% for you?

Your Notes:

Chapter Twelve

Persuasion

"Thoughts lead on to purposes; purposes go forth in action; actions form habits; habits decide character; and character fixes our destiny."
-Tryon Edwards

Let's start with an adage. "Persuasion works best when you are invited in." All around us we are being influenced. Influence and persuasion have two foundations. The foundation of external influence and one of internal influence.

It is the internal one which makes the biggest impression on us. This internal pressure is in the form of desire to have a particular product or service. Buying is very emotive. Selling is nothing but the transference of emotions. You make different buying decisions when you are in a certain mood. Have you ever been shopping for something you wanted and were in the wrong state of mind?

You show me a born seller and I will show you a born buyer. If you get me in the right state of mind and talk to me in my language on my wavelength and present it the right way for me and you are compelling, I don't care who you are or what you are selling, I will buy it!

We love buying. Of course we do. Even in challenging times people will still buy.

Often I get to hear "I'm not a sales person Jamie." The fact is that whether you know it or not you are. We are always selling something to someone. The idea to the board, the product or service to someone else, if you are married or have a significant other we are selling ourselves in a relationship. Your kids are 'selling' when they want you to do something. In fact they are some of the best influencers on the planet.

Emotion v Logic

Firstly you have to understand that the mind doesn't work on logic. If it did smoking would have been a thing of the past because where is the logic in having a huge sign on the front of a packet of cigarettes saying "smoking kills' and then continuing to smoke?

If you smoke that is your choice. But there is no logic to it. What would shift that thinking to the 'manager' or the unconscious mind is if it read "SMOKING KILLS YOU" With the emphasis on YOU. It does get one in three but the logical mind says "I won't be one of them."

Anticipated Regret

In 2006 I was in Palm Springs with my wife and met a very successful Hollywood agent called Stephen. We were discussing peak performance in business and the mindset he wanted to have. He said that he had mastered most things in his life but desperately wanted to give up smoking saying that he had tried everything. The patches, alternative therapies such as hypnosis and others. I could not resist rising to the occasion so I said "you've tried everything?"

"Yes, everything, I just cant give it up."

"Have you got any children?" I asked to which he replied no.

"Who do you have that you love, any children in your extended family?" He said he had a niece and nephew that he adored.

"Imagine Steve, that your beautiful niece is at your funeral watching, looking at you. You can see the pain in her face because her Uncle has passed away because of years of smoking." I continued, "or better still imagine that she comes to you on a different occasion, and says "I only started smoking because Uncle Stephen smoked."

A few months later I received an email from Stephen just touching base and he added: "I have not smoked for three months now. People ask me all the time how did I do it. I tell them that this guy in Manchester got me to imagine being at my own funeral and seeing my niece. I have not smoked for three months."

Now that is extreme and I wouldn't normally do that with a client or anyone else but he said he'd tried everything. That was the problem. Trying. There is no such thing. If I asked you to *try* and pick up a chair you would lift it immediately. I would then say, "No you just picked it up. Try and pick it up."

Another confused look and then you would stand

and look at me as though I was mad.

"Now you are not picking it up. *Try* and pick it up."

Trying is when you have both hands on the chair and you are not doing anything.

"You are either picking the chair up or you are not. Try does not exist!"

What are you trying to do in your life, business, or sports career? Are you trying to get better, improve your technique, are you trying to start a business? If a friend tells you they will try and make it to the party, what do you know? They are not making it.

Ultimately I wanted Stephen to connect with the manager. He had been talking to the front desk. When you talk to the front desk you end up in the loop of insanity, frustrated because of those actions which are not getting the results you are after.

The four questions in the mind of the other person when this happens are:

1. Do you really have my best interest in mind or are you here for a sale or your own interests?
2. What is this, what's in it for me and can you prove it?
3. Will it really give me what I want and need?
4. Do I really need it now?

Resistance: The Brick Wall

There is something called the Trained Brain Sandwich (and no, you cannot eat it). There are three aspects to the sandwich: The two layers of bread and the filler (it is a very traditional sandwich.).

It's made up of:
TRUST: The top layer.
BULLSEYE QUESTIONS: The filler.
STATE: The bottom layer.
I know you want to know more so let's go take a closer look at it.

1. TRUST:

This can be gained in several ways. The mind is making decisions of whether it likes you or not within the first seven seconds. That's how quickly we pick things up, we sense it. All you are looking for with the person in front, with a player or any human being in any normal situation is to connect at a deeper level. You will have done this or seen it in a restaurant where two people seem to be in sync with each other. They seem to be speaking at the same time, they seem to be moving in sync. How they feel is very important and their movements are synchronised. That is the quickest way to get into the other person's world. To put your body in sync. When the body is in sync the words will follow. This process is called matching and mirroring.

Trust can also be had from the way that you use your words. The tonality, the speed in which you speak and the pitch you speak. The tonality represents 38% of how effectively you communicate and it stems from your words as well as the tone of these words.

Visual

Imagine what's it like when you have someone in

front of you and they speak very quickly. Almost as though the words in their head are flashing across the screen of their mind. They can't get their words out fast enough and their hands are gesturing at a rate of knots.

The opposite can be true. That person may have a tendency to talk very slowly, they are tuned into their feelings more than processing their world through images. They say things like:

"It just doesn't make sense to me."
"I can't grasp that."
"You are taking that to heart."

All of these are words which describe that they are in the channel of kinesthetics. When there are two people in different channels they often say to themselves that they are on different wavelengths. One is saying to the other...."will you slow down." And the other is saying...."Jeez, will you speed up."

There is also the auditory channel. This channel is one where the person is tuned into the sounds. They use words and phrases such as the ones below:

"That rings true."
"I like the sound of that."
"Explain it again to me."

They use the words that are sensory rich in that channel. Have a look at the list below with some phrases and words that will help you identify what channel the person you are communicating with is tuned into.

Today, listen and gather. Most people don't listen but stay in their head talking to themselves or repeating what they will say. Listen before asking a question. Making contact at the unconscious level can be instant. Remember 7% of how effective your communication is words so 93% is communicated through body and tonality.

Have a look at the following list of words and phrases that you *MUST* listen out for to decipher the channel that the person in front of you is tuned into.

Key point: They can flip channels at any time. No one is always tuned into one channel. If you want to listen to the live sport on the radio you don't listen to Jazz FM. If you want to listen to international news you don't tune into the local station you find the BBC World service. By listening carefully you ensure that you are always in tune with the other person.

Have a look at the list below of some phrases and words. These are known as predicates or sensory rich words that help identify the channel.

PREDICATE LIST

VISUAL

Attractive	Foresee	Reveal
Blurred	Picture	Vivid
Twinkle	View	Perspective
Colourful	Flash	Visualize
Glow	Sparkle	Exhibit
Clear	Look	Preview
Obscure	Staring	Sightsee
Imagine	Graphic	Illuminate

AUDITORY

Manner of speaking
To tell the truth
Hold your tongue
State your purpose
Voice of reason
Rings a bell
Unheard of
Hidden messages
Give me your ear
Blabber mouth
Purrs like a kitten
Word for word

KINESTHETIC

Pull some strings
Pain in the neck
Hold on
Slipped my mind
Get a load of this
Get in touch with
Get a handle on
Firm foundation
Floating on air

If you are to improve your persuasion skills you need to develop an ear for the channel they are communicating in so you can mirror back to them the words and the tonality. Throw in the ability to match the body language and you will start to tune into their wavelength.

In order to tune in you have to become interested in people not attempting to be interesting.

Remember: Be *interested* not interesting.

This will reduce the amount of resistance you come across which makes it great for interviews, presentations, networking events and even dating.

Filler: The filler in the trained brain sandwich are the No Bull Questions. The quality of the questions you ask yourself and others has been fundamental in communication. These phrases are important because they do a couple of things.

1. They bypass the conscious mind so they are covert in hitting the bullseye.

2. They light up the movie mind meaning that the person has to access and talk to the manager in order to answer the question.

BULLSEYE PHRASES: Keys To The Door Of The Unconscious Mind

• "Have you ever......"

Three words that can produce magic, literally! To ask a person "have you ever" is actually commanding them to go inside and remember when they did, re-experiencing all those feelings! A powerful, no, make that a super-powerful way to induce states and trigger internal processes. "Have you ever experienced incredible excitement, thinking about mastering new skills?""Have you ever played well?" This isn't positive thinking or pumping yourself up. If I am coaching an athlete who is struggling it's one of the first questions that I ask them. Why? In order to answer that question you have to access the movie mind. You have to go back to a specific time. If the business executive is stressed the question is "Have you ever been relaxed?"

Ask three people a question that starts with this bullseye phrase. Then watch and listen to their response. Notice a change in their facial expressions as they begin to access the library of mental DVD's. Then ask them "did you put a picture of the time when you were X?"

- "What's it like when….."

Again here is a very powerful communication tool, very similar to the one above but no less effective. Asking "What's it like?" forces a person to go in and recall the circumstance, state or condition. "What's it like when you feel completely relaxed?"

"What's it like when you finish a big project?"
"What's it like when you are at your best?"
"What's it like when you go to your favourite retail store?"
Ask three people a question that starts with this phrase and calibrate their response.

- "When you……"

"When you" presupposes that you're going to do the aspect discussed or enter the state, so it is no longer open to debate. "When you get incredibly curious do you just find yourself compelled to act on it and find out?"

"When you perform to your ability do you find yourself feeling better about yourself?"

Ask three people a question that starts with this phrase and calibrate their response.

• "What would it be like if......"

This statement is in effect a command for the person to imagine the condition or occurrence named or described after it. "What would it be like if you owned this car?" "What would it be like to book us now?"

• "A person can...."

By talking about a "person's" experience it deflects any resistance on the part of your subject since you aren't really talking about *them*. "A person can go to a completely new level at golf by working on their mental game!"

• "If you were to...."

A really useful phrase! By saying "if" you are deflecting resistance while at the same time directing the person to imagine experiencing the condition, feeling or behaviour. "If you were to take a series of sessions..."

• "As you...."

This phrase presupposes the person will do the behaviour or undergo the experience. "As you grow more and more relaxed....."

This is a great example of negation.

Have you ever said to a child "Don't run or don't touch?" What do they end up doing? They run. Why because the mind doesn't process the word "don't". It will do everything after it. By saying your command "it's not necessary to" – it dissipates any resistance. "It's not necessary at this stage to hire me."

• "It's not necessary to...."

An example of negation by saying your command isn't necessary to – dissipates any resistance. "It's not necessary at this stage to hire me as a coach."

"It's not necessary at this stage to hire me."

• "You really shouldn't..."

Another negation pattern. Since your saying they shouldn't, it's not like you are trying to get them to do it! "You really shouldn't want this new jacket!"

• You might find yourself...

Useful as, the start of an intensifying chain of phrases. Implying that they are going to experience what you describe as something that just happens, so not only can they not resist it, but also it implies that you had nothing to do with it! You might find that a picture of you owning this house feeling those good feelings could appear in your mind."

• "Notice what it's like..."

Implies that the condition or experience is going to take place. Very useful for moving people's internal pictures. "Notice what it's like as you let go of the past and you replace it with a mindset that is going to move you forward with confidence."

• "What would it feel like if...."

Presumes the condition is going to take place plus is completely non-threatening as it uses "what if" – "What would it feel like if you were to instantaneously swing the putter with rhythm?"

"What would it feel like if you were to finish this on time?"

Internal v External

Here we are ready to take a look at the internal and external game of a leader: *THE DRIVING FORCES.*

How do you motivate those you are leading? Imagine your son or daughter are preparing for exams. Understanding whether they respond to the carrot or the stick can be the difference in them taking action towards their goals and objectives. Do they see something through or do they leave it until the last minute and want to change what they are doing?

We are all motivated by two driving forces. Every decision you or I make is driven by the need to AVOID PAIN or MOVE TOWARD PLEASURE. Said differently, you and I eat because we are hungry (avoiding pain) or we want to eat a certain food or at a certain restaurant because we like it (towards pleasure). That is logical enough.

A leader has an acute sensitivity to the motivation and action compass that is guiding those he or she is coaching. Not everyone has their compass pointing the same way in all contexts. It can change, which is why it is important not to consider this as just CARROT AND STICK.

There are subtle uses of language in this quadrant that can enhance peak performance or even hinder it.

I want you to go back to the time when your parents, guardian or mentors where helping you at a critical stage in your life. Maybe it was the transition from high school to college maybe it was a choice in career or taking on a new job. How did they push your buttons? How did you respond to them?

In this instant we will use the transition from high school to college and the preparation for the exams you had to take. Did they use one of the following two forms of communication?

1. If you don't study and you fail your exams you are going to be left behind and have to sit them again? Your friends will go on and leave you behind. Or did you recall something like the next example.

2. Passing your exams will give you many opportunities. You will have good qualifications that can lead to good jobs. That leads to increased salaries and you'll be able to holiday like Mum and Dad and have the nice big car to fit in your 2.4 kids.

The first one is clearly communication that is directed to AVOIDING PAIN whilst the second is MOVING TOWARDS PLEASURE. It is important that you know which one the person in front of you is driven by as assuming the wrong one can be costly and a drain on your emotional bank account.

I often ask a client "why do you do what you do?" That could be work related or even sports related. Then I listen intently to the answer, as it will have the clues to how they make their decisions which will then help me understand what motivates them.

Ask yourself the same question and without filtering the answer. Bring to mind now why do you do what you do?

"Why do you work?"

What comes to mind? What movies have started to play on your screen in your mind? What have you associated with the answer to that question? You may answer, "because I enjoy it" or you may answer "I have bills to pay." You may answer with a touch of both. As a leader or coach awareness of how you are motivating and communicating is important as much of your words could be falling on deaf ears.

Identify which of the two you have a tendency to associate with. Do you prefer the stick or the carrot? I say that because what's it like when someone you are working with, you want them to move onto some task and you just don't seem to get through to them or they can't find the time? Usually this comes down to the appropriate tweak in the pain or pleasure department. This isn't logical, as the unconscious mind doesn't operate on logic.

Look at the Western world in terms of advertising. It is primarily driven by pleasure. Drive this car and you will feel sexy, wear these clothes and you will look and feel like the film star of the moment. Most of our world is conditioned by pleasure. However there have been recent times where we have been responding to the influx of terrorism. Security has been driven by the need to avoid pain. Fear of loss. Governments in both the USA and the UK have played on this driving force. Policy has been guided by it, campaigns have been fueled with this most powerful of human tendencies.

We are hardwired from birth to avoid it. The protective mechanism within kicks in when the emotional part of the brain is triggered. So we will do much more to stop ourselves losing money than we will to gain it.

BULLSEYE COMMUNICATION: Are you on the right wavelength?

We say we are on the same wavelength as someone when we are communicating well with them and both feel we can understand each other. To be on the same wavelength as your performers you should calibrate and become aware of their tendencies.

Why do some people go to the gym and exercise? Some do it to stay in shape because if they were to sit around watching TV they would feel sluggish. Some however exercise because they want to look great and feel great. When I am coaching trainers on effective communication for their clients I highlight these tendencies because if you assume that everyone is doing exercise to feel good (pleasure) and you motivate everyone with the same message then those who are avoiding pain will feel angry at a deeper level. They will feel angry because they are not being understood. We all want to be understood. Empathy is an essential leadership quality but keep in mind that it is context related.

Leadership is an Internal Game

Again this is a context related issue but you should be aware of this tendency. How do you know you have done a good job? Is it that someone tells you, do you like feedback from a client? Is it when the company makes a healthy profit or is it that you feel the satisfaction, something on the inside lets you know?

Excellence requires a touch of both. A champion has a strong internal frame of reference. Think of great athletes, the superstars who make the back sports pages of newspapers. Federer, Woods, Jordan, McEnroe, Schumacher, Navratilova. All great champions who were focused on what they wanted to do. Interestingly though some of them handled being external better than others. For some it was more natural and others had to work at it.

Nick Faldo has over the past couple of years been developing his external side as he is the Ryder Cup captain in 2008 and that role will demand external qualities.

Leaders have both internal and external qualities. They have to have an external reference to be able to listen to advisers and those they lead. At the same time have the strength of conviction to believe in their own policies and decisions. If the leader had a very strong external reference they would be influenced by others and often be responding to their world or asking what others thought rather than creating their world.

When dealing with someone who seems very independent in his or her thinking I will always use this line in my coaching. It involves identifying the strong internal reference, someone who knows what they want. Someone who isn't convinced by an idea, a philosophy or who wants to do the task their way. This simple line of "There is only you that would know (internal reference) how useful this information will be to your career." I am on the same wavelength because unconsciously I am stating that I understand them. I am not telling them what to do.

To add something else to the mix I will continue "there is only you that knows who will miss out by not taking action." (A little pain to add to the moving away from reference).

I have worked with a premiership striker in England whose nature is external. He took this into his performances. A striker in front of a goal wants to have a strong internal reference. The feeling that "he knows" he is going to score. A midfielder or playmaker should have a strong external reference. Does that make sense? Ask your teams and individuals how do they know they have done a good job. What do they benchmark it by? As well as their behaviour you will find that they are showing tendencies in their actions to internal or external references.

Coaches, good coaches I might add have a strong external reference with a balance point of some internal. It is very similar to great leaders. There isn't a right or wrong. We all have a tendency to use one hand more than the other. Yet this doesn't stop us using either. Just be aware. Point out that an external reference should be balanced with being a little more focused or even selfish in some situations.

Your Notes:

Chapter Thirteen

The Pressure is on

"Are you bored with life? Then throw yourself into some work you believe in with all your heart, live for it, die for it, and you will find happiness that you had thought could never be yours."
-Audrey Hepburn

In sports like in life we have expectations that often keep us from reaching the heights that we aspire to. Some can deal with those expectations and some allow them to weigh them down. It's as common in school as it is in business as it is in sports. I just recently gave a talk to a group of 16 year olds who are taking their exams. I asked them what was the one area that they would like to deal with. "Expectations," they shouted almost all as one.

Pressure in life can either work for us and drive us towards our goals or it can work against us. I often say to someone when they say they are feeling pressure, that pressure is what you put in tyres. The whole language around what and how you communicate with yourself is what creates the perceived pressure.

I explained to the kids just as I have explained to you that there is a little game that is being played below the surface. The 'WWTTOM' game. This is an acronym of course. It means: "What Will They Think Of Me?" game.

Expectations are something which affect everyone. Some people can deal with them and others can't. Pat Riley the great NBA basketball coach would often use the phrase "Stop looking to play the excellent game. We need to develop game excellence."

He had a point. Small changes create an impact and this change is about switching the words around from excellent game to game excellence. The difference being that if you play well you feel really good. That is you feel like you really are playing at the top of your peak.

If you have a bad day you don't feel good. This is the problem because then you end up on the roller coaster of play well feel good. You walk into the clubhouse or the players' lounge and you find yourself thinking you are 'the man' or even 'man of the match'. That changes though when you haven't played well. You don't want to walk into the clubhouse in fact you just want to disappear. You are thinking how do I get back to that level because I don't know how I did it.

That up and down pattern is full of pain and frustration. The uncertainty is what riddles you.

Game Excellence is a different pattern. It is about a more consistent mindset. The upside isn't as steep as you are continually growing and stretching. Yes there will be a drop somewhere, you will lose a deal, you will miss an easy chance in a game, you will fail to make the cut in golf or even fail a test. But you know you will get back on track. You also know that your drop isn't as steep as the drop of looking for an excellent game. That is playing by other people's standards. You are constantly trying to impress them. In attempting to impress others you create the anxiety and the frustration in yourself which hampers you from performing well. The mind is always jumping into the past and the future. Craving to be in the present. Like the monkey mind as they call it in the East your emotions are all over the place.

Game excellence is consistent. You know you are going to get back on track. You play by your standards. They are rising. If they are not good enough for the environment you are in then you have to 'think differently'. The environment will demand that you raise your game or you will stay the same.

Real You v Performer You.

Your identity in sports, business and life can very often be attached to what you do. I said earlier that our jobs and environments give us those identities. If we catch onto them too much though through our ego they then shape our identity. Let's look at some classic examples:

"I'm a parent"

"I am a teacher"

"I am a millionaire"

"I am a football fan"

"I am a Doctor"

"I am homeless"

"I am…" Whenever you start or say with "I am.."

you are accessing the ego mind.

Yet you are none of those really. What you are is a son or daughter. You are maybe a significant other, you may be a fan of sports, you may be a cousin, brother or sister, you may be a parent, a father or mother. These are all about *who* you are. They are given. Your self worth as an individual cannot be taken. Though you can give it away. And it is often given away. Yet this is the *real you*.

The performer you

The performer you is what you do. If you play a sport, you work in business or you have a job or even you are in education. This is what you do.

The mental challenges become more intense, the pressure mounts and the expectations become harder to deal with when you take the real you into the event and cross the line. The real you cannot deal with the expectations, the real you cannot deal with the pressure, which is why you need the performer.

The Safe Place

Eldrick Woods started playing golf at the age of two. His parents wanted to create a safe place for him to find out how good he could become. There was no grand plan for him to become the best golfer ever, although that is the perception which has been popularly cultivated. His father Earl gave him the nickname 'Tiger' after a friend of his in the military.

His parents wanted Tiger to be able to play golf

from a safe place and protect his real self. So every time Eldrick stepped on the golf course he became Tiger.

If Tiger had a bad day on the golf course. He came back home and Eldrick was OK. Eldrick didn't all of a sudden become a grumpy, spoilt brat because he didn't play well. Likewise when Tiger had a good day on the golf course it didn't mean he was any better a son, or a friend because he had shot a good number or won the tournament.

The margin for failure is very small. If you play well and feel great and come home and your meal tastes so much better yet in defeat you come back and the same meal tastes dreadful and you are hard work to be around then you have succumbed to taking the real you into the environment of the performer.

I see this a lot in sports, all sports. Tennis, golf, cricket football, I see it in business, I see it with young people in exams. It affects minorities, it affects women and young women especially.

Who you are is a given. What you do is what you do and your whole being isn't attached to a ball or a number.

In adults this happens when you don't perform like you want to. You become frustrated and anxious about stepping over the line into the performer you. In fact who you really take is the real you into the event. The real you cannot deal with the expectations. The real you cannot handle the pressure.

Tiger can handle the pressure. Tiger can deal with the expectations. Michael Jordan would step on the court and transform himself into Air Jordan. Many famous peak performers have had the ability to go from real self to performer self.

Here are some examples of people you may have heard of:

Eldrick	Tiger (Golf)
Michael Jordan	Air Jordan (Basketball)
Jack Nichlaus	Golden Bear (Golf)
John McEnroe	The Brat (Tennis)
Pete Sampras	Pistol Pete (Tennis)
Katie Price	Jordan (Model)
Reggie Dwight	Elton John
Andrew Flintoff	Freddie
Lewis Moody	Crazy Horse
Peter Parker	Spiderman
Clark Kent	Superman

We all have a 'someone' a name that we were called when we were at our best. All of the above had the ability to change into that 'someone' who could get the job done for them.

When they transformed they were accessing that part of them that could handle or deal with anything the game or life threw at them.

Whenever I come across someone who is not at their best I often wonder if they have taken the real them into work or into the big game.

The Pressure Gauge is measured by numbers. You react to what the reading is giving you and in many contexts of peak performance pressure is measured by numbers. You can either deal with the numbers or you can't. In sports the number is score lines, in business it is number of sales, profit/loss, targets, salary and so on.

Whenever we put so much importance on scores I

refer to it as Symbolic Importance of the Number or (SION). There are many sports where the individual can be carrying the burden of the Symbolic Importance of Numbers. Footballers do it with the large transfers that are attached to them. They put importance on the price tag. Yet when they played months before and there was no talk of a move they were fine performing with freedom. But the "SION" has contributed to justifying the price tag. The young crop of tennis players I work with at the All England Club all have ratings that determine their level of performance. What most players do is look at the draw to see who they will be playing. They then look at their opponents rating and then put pressure on themselves that they have to win or they should win. This observation is based on the number. Yet they do not take into consideration what game they will show up with on the day.

The only criteria you have control of is yourself. Unlike other sports you have the opportunity to dictate the tempo, have the opponent running all over the court, your team has the ability to steal the ball back.

There are some sports such as downhill mountain bike riding, golf, running or individual sports that you have no impact on your opponent by physically involving yourself in their endeavour. Yet in the quest to perform well the athlete will put unnecessary pressure on themselves before the clock starts to tick because of the Symbolic Importance of the Number.

"I have to post this time, run this, shoot this score." When you look closer it is because they are playing the games below the surface. Their real self is in conflict with the performer and is trying to impress.

By no means am I saying that you don't have targets, goals and dreams. I have already mentioned that measuring progress is evidence for the mind and writing it down is important. But I want you to consider these two clubs we will look at next.

The Forecast Club

This club is such a popular members' club that it is almost oversubscribed. Forecasting is what the weather anchors do. "Today over the north west we will experience dry spells and the temperature will rise to three degrees later in the afternoon." So you go with the forecast and don't take your jacket. Not a good move in the north west of England. Especially in the rainy city of Manchester. It rains in the afternoon and now you feel stupid because you forecast the weather or listened to the forecasters. In professional sports, especially football, the pundits call the score of the big games of the weekend. More often than not they forecast and it doesn't go the way they predicted.

Forecasting creates anxiety. Uncertainty that works against you. "I am supposed to beat this guy. I am supposed to close this deal out. They are supposed to finish the year with x."

The Exclusive Club

Let's look at the other club now. It has fewer members. It is a little more exclusive.

Write these initials down on a notepad, on a postcard as a reminder: The 'LSWH' Club otherwise known as The 'Let's See What Happens' Club. When you approach your event, situation, game, with the mindset of 'Let's See What Happens' you stay away from the forecasting of results and the negative feelings that go with them. In fact you bring on a state of calm, a more relaxed and focused approach that keeps you in the moment. So when you go against someone who is by definition ranked, graded at another level, leave the forecasting to the weatherman. You do not know what game they are going to bring.

A client told me "I feel like I am going to play well though." Yes that is good and your preparation gives you confidence. But when you think you *should* beat someone just because of the number you have, or even the league position then you are drawn into the uncertain world of forecasting and uncertainty induces anxiety and problems.

This applies to life too. How often have you forecast that something isn't going to come off?

"I won't get this job."

"I will get this job."

"We are going to get the deal."

It's all forecasting. Join the 'Let's See What Happens' Club' and notice the difference in how you take on your projects.

Dealing with it

Depending upon where and who you have been coached by or spent much of your upbringing or professional life with, will determine how you deal with adversity in sports, business and life. The culture you have been brought up will have an impact on your attitude towards failure. For many in business who have become the household names of global business have been driven by a need to avoid failure. Many have been on the brink of failure and then there are those who embrace it.

The communication with yourself is critical in challenging times. Without you realising it, your conscious mind can rant and rave about the lack of opportunities and the constant pressure to make things happen.

Your relationship with yourself is what gets you through the tough times. The belief that you can get across the finish line despite what is happening in the world.

Who do you know who has bounced back from adversity in sports, business or life? Right before you in the news, in books, there are stories of triumph over adversity. People who have recovered from some positions so precarious that you wouldn't have thought they could possibly have recovered from, but they did.

One of my personal favourites is that of Garrett Porter. At nine years of age he had been diagnosed as having an inoperable brain tumor. It was a right-hemisphere brain tumor, and his prognosis was that he had less than a year to live. A CAT scan revealed that his tumor had grown considerably and no further medical treatment was indicated. He was sent home with no hope but a meeting with Dr. Patricia Norris who in 1978 had been pioneering self regulation and healing with her clients using meditation and bio feedback with visualization techniques.

At the time *Star Wars* was the film of the moment and Garrett was a huge fan. She had him create this personal crusade against the enemy where he imagined the white bloods cells zapping the cancerous tumour. Every day and night he went on his mission as the flight squadron leader visualizing the battle against the alien invader in his brain. After working with Dr. Norris for six months, Garrett went back for a CAT scan and to the medics' surprise there was no sign of the tumour but a small black shadow on the screen. They were so surprised to find no trace of the disease that they asked if he had had it surgically removed. The second CAT scan confirmed his "knowingness." It had gone!

There are countless stories like Garrett's. His is not only one of resolve and determination but a story that has utilized the dynamics of creating images and clarity of intention using the mind. In sports the use of imagery is well documented. Garrett had the tools in his kit bag to deal with what had been thrown at him.

So what's the mindset for dealing with failure? In sports business and life it's the management of failure. Well in the earlier chapter I talked about the code word of *possible*. This concept does keep you present to your experience it will not allow you to drift into the future and it doesn't allow you to visit the past of what went wrong. Imagine Garrett Porter not having that resolve and mindset.

"What might happen?"

"Why has this happened to me?" These are questions that do come up. He had the mindset of dealing with whatever his circumstances threw at him.

How Big Is Your Hero?

I'm not an avid film goer but I do have some favourites and old classics. We become mesmerized, our attention captured by good films because the main character goes through some transformation in his or her own life that pits them against some greater power that wants to hold them back.

Every storyline has three elements to it. The character is being challenged by one of if not all of the following elements.

EXTERNAL: There is an EXTERNAL conflict or enemy. Some organisation or person who wants to break down the main character in your film.

INTERNAL: In every film the character has an internal conflict. Resolving some internal weakness, overcoming a failing somewhere in his or her life.

Just like in many of your favourite films you have a main character that throughout the film is going through some struggle.

INTIMATE: Then there is an intimate opponent that our character has to face. That could be a lover, a relative, or a friend. There is always an intimate opponent.

As you think about the story of your own life now which one do you relate with? Are you going up against an external opponent. A manager, an organisation? What is it you are fighting with? Are you fighting and repeating the same patterns? Can you find another place or way to resolve this than the way you are going about it presently?

What is the internal opponent that you are facing today?

What is the intimate challenge or opponent that you are up against? Family, friends, your significant other?

So what will your story be?

The bigger the opponent the bigger the hero has to be.

There is no such thing as failure

What if you never failed? What if there was a belief that it was all learning. Depending on your own thinking and how you apply it to your world will depend on how you look at the inevitable topic of the 'F' word.

What if it was developing you for the moment you are in? Where you find yourself now. That the lesson in that event, loss, mistake made you stronger for the next event, moment or even chapter in your life?

Mistakes are worth making. It's called learning. The ability to read and write came from mistakes: The codeword for learning.

Yet ask young people about mistakes and they freeze with terror at the thought. Sport is the same. Make mistakes. Learn quickly and move on. The new president of America, Barack Obama. said it like this:

"I'm not looking for anyone who has never made a mistake," because he knows there are people in government who have made mistakes. He said he wouldn't be where he was, the position to lead his country if he hadn't made mistakes along the way.

It's the mistakes you keep making that are the ones you want to avoid. The habitual ones.

One of the most celebrated athletes in modern

history and the greatest basketball player of his generation said it like this: "I've missed more than 9000 shots in my career. I've lost almost 300 games, 26 times, I've been trusted to take the game winning shot and missed. I've failed over and over and over again in my life. And that is why I succeed." It was the basketball legend, Michael Jordan.

So when faced with challenging times start asking yourself better questions to shift your perception of what failing and mistakes are. If the theme of this book has been anything it has been about the quality of the questions that you ask.

Start by adding these to a piece of card and train yourself to start sentences and thinking with the following:

How can I....?

What Can I ....?

Who can I .....?

Where can I ....?

You get to ask good questions by repetition; through practice you become accustomed to starting sentences with the above. Sports and life are interchangeable. Practice makes perfect in either field.

Your Notes:

Chapter Fourteen

Purpose

"The strongest principle of growth lies in the human choice."
-George Eliott

Why do we do what we do? Why do you do what you do? This is a question that we either find the answer to or we end up searching for a good while. Many of the great books or philosophers of our time have often referred to or made reference to all of us being here for a purpose. The goal in life is to find out what that purpose is and then to honour it. So why in a book on peak performance do I discuss why you are here?

You cannot be or operate in a Peak State if you do not have a purpose, if you are not fully engaged and are not sure why you are here.

Many people have been put here for a reason. In fact everyone has been put here for a reason. When I am working with a client who is experiencing poor form in their sport then I have a good idea that they have lost a certain passion for what they do. That energy and desire that had been so much an important part of their development up to that point has started to elude them, thus causing them much anxiety and frustration.

It's worth remembering: tough times don't last tough people do.

So when you have times in which you question what you are doing and why, it helps to recall why you started doing what you do in the first place.

Think of a block with three levels. At the base of the block, is the basic survival level where work needs to be done and people want to be paid. We have to meet that comfort need. Then the middle block represents success. The question that you ask at this level is can I be successful doing what I am doing now? You will always seek the ability to improve where you are now.

Finally, at the top level you also want to transform your thinking from where you are. The transforming is the process of the self actualizing and improving. When you are at this level you can find why you are here. What is your calling.

For instance, are you wired to coach children football? Are you wired to do deals, to sell or are you wired to teach? Ask yourself what am I wired to do?

In the best selling book by Rick Warren *The Purpose Driven Life* his opening line was. "It's not about you." Life is about we and contribution. What on earth are you put here for?

Without getting too deep into this subject I feel that elite athletes always find their best performances when they stop going after the goal and start focusing on how much they are growing, stretching and contributing. That in itself leads to peak performance.

The renowned psychologist, Mihaly Csikzszentmihalyi says in his book *Flow: The psychology of Optimal Experience,* that "...how people respond to stress determines the quality of their lives, which is as close as any of us can come to being happy."

The Pressure is on

We all have a Professional and Spiritual Calling. Finding them is the challenge but sometimes they can be staring you in the face. The professional calling is what you love to do. Why you were put here for. What are you exceptional at? If you find your professional calling it is often something that you would do for free. Spiritual calling is by the same token what can you add to the proposal of work and giving.

As a 15 year old I had always had two mentors in my basketball career. Cleave Lewis was one of the under-appreciated American basketballers to come to the UK. It was a couple of years ago that we had the chance to play golf and catch up on many of the conversations that we often had as a youngster. Then last week he called me out of the blue to see how his protégé was getting on. In a moment of synchronicity I started to explain what I was up to.

"Cleave, I still can't believe.." and before I could finish the sentence he added, "how mentally weak people are?"

It was like I had just age-regressed to 15 years old and he was giving me a pearl of wisdom. The one thing he drummed into me was mental strength, determination on the basketball court and thinking differently.

In the tough times that are facing the world today the place to shift your attention is to others. There is always someone worse off than you and gratitude is an emotion that is needed in these days.

Ask yourself everyday, remind yourself "What am I grateful for in my life right now?"

It is very easy to overlook what we do have, who we do have in our life. The question that Rick Warren asked was "what is in your hands?"

Whatever you do you have something in your hands some skill or talent that you have been given to do something with to make a difference in the world.

For me it was basketball. The ball was in my hands. I used basketball and the skills of coaching as my influence on young people, that is my contribution, it gave me the tools to give peak performance coaching.

Income: My coaching at *trained brain* represents my career, my purpose. Your career represents what you do for a living and how you receive your income.

Identity: The job, career you have chosen represents the identity you have. You are a doctor, coach, teacher, banker, footballer. Whatever your profession your identity is represented at a level by what you are doing with your profession. Is this your professional calling? Are you doing what you are wired to do?

Are you living your spiritual calling? Is it about you? Or are you giving up yourself?

Remember that no matter what you do or who you are, your level of contribution to the world, to your community will be dictated by how much you grow as a person.

Your Notes:

Chapter Fifteen

Shape the future

"Ninety-nine percent of the failures come from people who have the habit of making excuses."
-George Washington Carver

We don't like change. Human beings are not comfortable with change. Yet we know we need to change in some context be it sports, business or life. There was a time when I used to say that everyone is designed for success. Again, the definitions of success can vary greatly. However, I stopped saying it because I learned that whilst opportunities present themselves in many guises for everyone we are designed as human beings to be comfortable. The other mind loves the comfort of patterns, it loves and craves knowing, its code word is certainty.

It loves knowing what will come next. If you want to stand out in your industry or field comfort doesn't get you on that road. It's not comfortable if you want to go up the corporate ladder and you commit to higher education, you return home from a hard day at the office and then have to hit the books. Comfort is sitting on the sofa flicking through the channels when you know you should be doing something more productive. It's not comfortable starting your own business in the early days. It's not comfortable being a World Champion or the best in your field because if it were everyone would be at that level.

The emphasis is on adding another dimension to what you do. It's finding out what your sauce is and where you can apply it.

Squares to triangles

Draw yourself a square on a piece of paper. Then next to it draw a triangle. And next to the triangle draw a circle. Now if those shapes were people and they were to be as curious as we humans are they would want to explore the new ideas, beliefs and attitudes that the other embodies. So the square would be very curious about the mindset of the circle and the triangle. Inevitably, after trying the triangle life and the way of the circle, our square resorts back to being a square. He tried to change but couldn't.

When a square finds it's own mental ketchup it adds another dimension to what it is doing. It is adding depth and therefore becomes a cube. When the triangle adds it's peak performance sauce again it has depth and becomes a pyramid. Finally, the circle, expands, adds depth and becomes a sphere.

They don't have to be like anyone else or change what they are. Instead what they have added is that dimension that makes you expand, allows you to stand out. Allows you to deal with what is thrown at you because you have added depth. You have a trained brain with trained skills you can tap into. That is the sauce of peak performance and it is what you have been learning throughout this book.

Trained Brain Triangle

Imagine a triangle with the word *ENJOYMENT* in the bottom left corner and the word *LEARNING* in the bottom right corner of the shape. At the top you can imagine the word *RESULTS*. Most of us live and work in a results business. Even down to the education arena. Today young people are thinking about results from an early age. The debate on competition in schools and with our future generations continues to raise questions about performance and how to bring up children. Their environment is based on performance and yet there hasn't been a great understanding of bouncing back installed in their hardware when they are younger nor an attempt to help them have the ingredients necessary to bounce back. It only seems occasional and is triggered by external stimulus or others. It's an internal philosophy. Have you ever come across this situation even if you don't play the sport?

Two golfers meet each other for the first time they don't know how the other plays golf. What's the first thing that they ask? What's your handicap?

What's the valid question there? Am I better than you or are you better than me? True?

Where is that question directed to on that triangle? Results, performance.

You come in off the golf course what's the first thing you get asked about in the club house? How did you do? Where is that directed? Results.

This is how it works:

If your triangle is out of balance you will experience pain and frustration. If your triangle is in balance you will have an optimal experience.

Now Jonny Miller the great golfer said when he was younger that "I would have had to be a fool not to be a great golfer; my father asked me two questions every time I came off the golf course. He asked me what did you enjoy today son and what did you learn?"

If your brain gets asked those two questions every time you do something, what's it going to look for? Enjoyment and what it has learnt.

Like most sports or hobbies there is a steep learning curve, tons of learning, stretching your ability and growing as a result. This very process of constantly being stretched leads to you loving the process. That's enjoyment. In fact going back to golfers, when they started playing just seeing the damn thing in the air was enough to have them coming back for more. So what happened?

Results is what happened. From really enjoying the process of learning the focus was shifted to scores. They get dragged into the top part of the triangle. In business and life results are very important yet not without looking at how they are being attained. I have seen many an executive who has burned out, a sales person who has lost confidence or a player who has lost their touch due to the Symbolic Importance of the Number (SION). This is the route to pain and frustration. It also leads to anxiety tipping the triangle out of balance.

Ask yourself, "Is my triangle in balance?"

Is your triangle in balance in other areas of your life?

What can you enjoy about your professional life that you have overlooked?

Why did you start in that profession? What could you enjoy?

There are many aspects to what we do from working with people, colleagues, the deal, the service. Whatever it may be there is something that you can find. If you have stopped learning and enjoying the chances are the performance and results are going to suffer.

The Quarter Shot Effect

You are never really looking for a massive change in something to get exponential results. It is usually that small shift in thinking and actions that create momentum for you. One of my close friends and colleagues in Munich Justin Walsh works with many European stars and one in particular is rising German golf star and Ladies European Tour player Martina Eberl. In 2006 she engaged Trained Brain to develop her mental skills. During the 2006 season her scoring average was 73.5 and finished 47th in the order of merit. The following year 2007 she improved to average 72.9 and finished the season 9th best in Europe. A 0.6 change in her performances and continued that improvement in the 2008 season by averaging 72.55. So in total over three years she went to from 73.5 to 72.55 a difference of a shot. Only one shot that catapulted her from 47th to 3rd in the European rankings propelling her to the status of one of Europe's leading future stars. Her work with Justin was underpinned by the 0.25 of a shot a round over the season they worked towards. In fact a quarter of a shot was calculated to move her from 35th to 10th. Small changes can have big results. What is the quarter of a shot in your world that could make such an impact? Committing to new learnings and committing to enjoying what you do can be that quarter of a shot. When that happens you will find that the results take care of themselves.

As you come to the end of the book you will find that many of these concepts are very practical in both understanding and in application. There comes a point when understanding has to be put on the back burner. This is a problem in society today because many understand but do not do.

The difference is in between knowing and doing. The difference between knowing what to do and doing what you know. "It's obvious really" is often the comment. "Common sense." It is common sense.

Common sense is only common sense if it is based upon common experience. Now you have been exposed to the same sauce that I have coached to some of the best at what they do. Taking action whilst reading this book helps you to create momentum.

You will never have a problem that you don't have the resources to deal with. Someone somewhere has had your challenge. Get resourceful. Let go of the illusion that you have to be in pain to achieve. We are going through some of the most challenging times in the history of the world.

"Play as though it is the last two minutes of your world cup final." I remember hearing a mentor add to his words. What he meant was really live and play in every minute as though you were going to play your last game. Richard Bandler one of the founding fathers of practical psychology and still a leading light in neurolinguistics said that "We think we are eternal. That this will go on for ever."

In making his own history the newly elected President Barack Obama had to be asking good questions. Was America ready for him? He asked why not?

Then more importantly he would have added to that. Why not me?

What is the internal dialogue you are having with yourself?

What are you asking?

Sometimes asking the questions that lead us to clarity about where we are and where we want to be come down to the lenses we are looking through. If those lenses have been distorted by the brown in life then you will see the world through those eyes.

"A change in perspective will change a barren wasteland into a field of opportunity."

This poem I was sent by a friend. It reminded me that our experiences of life are always relative and if we look through the lenses of life that are covered in mud then our view becomes distorted.

Sometimes we have to wipe away the _____ (you fill in the blank!) and really appreciate the opportunities, the people, the places, the loved ones we have. In many cases, gratitude is the emotion that melts away fear and uncertainty. Without being all fluffy it is well worth thinking about it for a moment.

When you become grateful and appreciative of what you have you melt the need to want what you don't have. It's called the present moment. It brings you back to this moment that is the only one that matters. You catch yourself being present. The memory of the past evokes feelings of gratitude.

Ask yourself today....
What am I grateful for in my life today?
Who am I grateful for having in my life today?
What opportunities am I grateful for today?

You Are Blessed
If you woke up this morning
With more health than illness,
You are more blessed than the
Million who won't survive the week.

If you have never experienced
the danger of battle,
the loneliness of imprisonment,
the agony of torture or
the pangs of starvation,
you are ahead of 20 million people
around the world.

If you attend a church meeting
without fear of harassment,
arrest, torture, or death,
you are more blessed than almost
three billion people in the world.

If you have food in your refrigerator,
clothes on your back, a roof over
your head and a place to sleep,

you are richer than 75% of this world.

If you have money in the bank,
in your wallet, and spare change
in a dish someplace, you are among
the top 8% of the world's wealthy.

If your parents are still married and alive,
you are very rare, especially in the United States.

If you hold up your head with a smile
on your face and are truly thankful,
you are blessed because the majority can,
but most do not.

If you can hold someone's hand, hug them
or even touch them on the shoulder,
you are blessed because you can
offer God's healing touch.

If you can read this message,
you are more blessed than over
two billion people in the world
that cannot read anything at all.

You are so blessed in ways
you may never even know.

Remember that the source of peak performance is within you. Not something that you can look for outside yourself. It is never far. All it takes is the touch of the right button, the changing of the channel. If you never press the button or ask yourself what is on the other side you will never know. Always ask yourself what if I do this differently? Ask a different question? If I just add this way of thinking to this area of my life that I haven't even considered it then I could experience a difference in what I am doing.

Remember that human beings rarely like to experience change is sports business or life. This isn't about changing who you are but adding another dimension to what you do in all areas of your life. My challenge to you is to be aware of the quality of your thinking. Be guarded with your PIN number to that emotional bank account. Make sure you are depositing everyday. The best way to ingrain anything new is to go and coach it to someone else. Share it with a friend, a child, colleague or a family member because when you share an idea you experience the lessons again with every message you send. I have been inspired by many in my life who have shared their stories with me from all walks of life, ages, backgrounds and professions.

If you just get one idea from spending time with this book which adds to your game then I consider myself to be very lucky to have shared some of the ideas and skills that have helped many others find and use their sauce.

"In-joy"

Jamie

Your Notes:

Jamie Edwards

Jamie Edwards is one of Europe's leading peak performance coaches. An identity he has established through his ability to help athletes, coaches and organisations create the results they aspire to.

His work has been tested at the highest levels of the sports such as the Rugby World Cup, the Ashes, Ryder Cup, World Cup Skiing, Extreme Sports and the Premiership and provides mental training for players at the All England Tennis Club.

He provides coaching for a range of athletes and coaches, his company Trained Brain has worked with World Cup rugby winner Lewis Moody MBE, Ashes heroes Freddie Flintoff & Michael Vaughan, Ryder Cup stars Lee Westwood and Darren Clarke, Paul McGinley, Graeme McDowell, WRC driver Guy Wilkes and several outstanding young Premiership footballers, and world champion downhill mountain bike team, Atherton Racing.

He has delivered workshops and lectured at a number of renowned universities such as Manchester, Loughborough and Oxford and is frequently called upon educators to provide training, keynote addresses and seminars across the country.

In the business arena Jamie works with a select number of Managing Director's and senior executives to assist with raising their own game beyond the numbers. His work has led him to consult with companies in a diverse number of fields such as leisure, software, telecommunications, direct sales, the MOD, entertainment and local government.

Corporate clients include Challenger World,

Adidas Group, Bombardier, Fortis, Investec, Sainsburys, Red Bull, Nokia, Gleneagles, Premier Global, Volvo, IBM, Marriott, BMW, Wentworth Club and Skibo Castle amongst others who have benefited from his knowledge of human technology.

Share your ketchup on twitter.com/jamieedwards

Visit our website: http://www.trained-brain.com/

Peak-performance self-development courses in audio and DVD

You can book Jamie to speak at your conferences and team events, or to coach your senior decision makers.

Tel: +44 (0) 1457 877 722
Email: info@trained-brain.com
Web: www.trained-brain.com

Your Notes

Your Notes